ANCIENT AFRICA

Ancient Africa

A GLOBAL HISTORY, TO 300 CE

Christopher Ehret

PRINCETON UNIVERSITY PRESS

PRINCETON & OXFORD

Published by Princeton University Press
41 William Street, Princeton, New Jersey 08540
99 Banbury Road, Oxford OX2 6JX

press.princeton.edu

All Rights Reserved

Library of Congress Cataloging-in-Publication Data

Names: Ehret, Christopher, 1941– author.
Title: Ancient Africa : a global history, to 300 CE / Christopher Ehret.
Description: Princeton : Princeton University Press, [2023] |
    Includes bibliographical references and index.
Identifiers: LCCN 2022028073 (print) | LCCN 2022028074 (ebook) |
    ISBN 9780691244099 (hardback) | ISBN 9780691244105 (ebook)
Subjects: LCSH: Africa—Civilization. | Africa—History—To 1498.
Classification: LCC DT14 .E35 2023 (print) | LCC DT14 (ebook) |
    DDC 960/.1—dc23/eng/20220616
LC record available at https://lccn.loc.gov/2022028073
LC ebook record available at https://lccn.loc.gov/2022028074

British Library Cataloging-in-Publication Data is available

Editorial: Priya Nelson, Barbara Shi, and Emma Wagh
Production Editorial: Theresa Liu
Jacket/Cover Design: Katie Osborne
Production: Danielle Amatucci
Publicity: Alyssa Sanford and Kate Farquhar-Thomson
Copyeditor: Beth Gianfagna

Front cover images: (*Top*) Zande throwing knife and (*middle*) flange-welded double bell photographed by Christopher Ehret. (*Bottom*) *Spindle whorl*. New Kingdom, Ramesside. Dynasty 19–20. ca. 1295–1070 BC. From Egypt, Memphite Region. Courtesy of the Rogers Fund and Edward S. Harkness Gift, 1922 / Metropolitian Museum of Art.

Backflap image: Black and red burnished ware from the Badarian in Middle Egypt. Courtesy of the Petrie Museum of Egyptian Archaeology.

This book has been composed in Miller (Classic)

Printed on acid-free paper. ∞

Printed in the United States of America

10 9 8 7 6 5 4 3 2

To two inspiring teachers,

Henry G. Dittmar and
Oswald Werner

In memoriam,

Shiferaw Alemu Assefa,
groundbreaking scholar of early African history

CONTENTS

ACKNOWLEDGMENTS

A LONG PERSONAL, as well as academic, history lies behind the writing of this book, and a great number of scholars and their work over the years have contributed to the shaping of the ideas and conclusions presented in this work.

I am especially indebted to the teachers who guided me in broadening and deepening my acquaintance with and skills in the use of multiple, cross-disciplinary sources for uncovering our deeper human past. Professor Henry G. Dittmar, a historian of Europe and the Ottoman Empire, created my undergraduate university's first African history course, introducing his students, among other things, to oral sources for history. I then had the good fortune of attending Northwestern University for my PhD studies. The African studies program there emphasized interdisciplinary exploration, and the history department proved ready to countenance the work of a postgraduate student who applied that cross-disciplinary range of expertise to historical studies. The anthropologist Oswald Werner trained me in the methods of reconstructing past cultural history from comparative ethnographic and linguistic evidence; the noted archaeologist Bruce Trigger was my mentor in archaeological method; and the linguist Professor Jack Berry completed my training in African historical and comparative linguistics. In addition, through an interuniversity program I had the privilege of studying with Professor Jan Vansina of the University of Wisconsin, a prolific scholar and founding figure in the use of oral tradition and an early leader in combining ethnographic, linguistic, and oral sources in the writing of African history.[1]

My debt is equally great to Professor Bethwell Allan Ogot, the dean of historians of eastern Africa, who encouraged and mentored me in my earliest African historical fieldwork, and to my longtime colleague Professor Merrick Posnansky, who over the years has repeatedly helped refine my understandings of archaeological resources.

Interactions with numerous other scholars, along with collaborative efforts over the years, have contributed in basic ways to the directions taken here in this book. These scholars include, inter alia, historians, anthropologists, linguists, archaeologists, biological anthropologists, geneticists, and students of rock art: Emmanuel K. Akyeampong, Nicholas J. Allen, Edward A. Alpers, Stanley H. Ambrose, David W. Anthony, Ofer Bar-Yosef, Peter Bellwood, the late M. Lionel Bender, Koen Bostoen, Steven A. Brandt, Alison Brooks, Graciela Cabana, Hilary Callan, Felix Chami, Shadreck Chirikure, David Christian, J. Desmond Clark, Nicholas David, James Denbow, Jared Diamond, Robin Dunbar, Ross Dunn, Edward Elderkin, Brian M. Fagan, François-Xavier Fauvelle, Elizabeth Fentress, Dorian Q. Fuller, the late Joseph Greenberg, Tom Güldemann, Randi Haaland, Michael Hammer, Fekri Hassan, Bernd Heine, Elisabeth Hildebrand, Augustin Holl, Mark Horton, Thomas Huffman, Eric Huysecom, Wendy James, Nicholas M. Katanekwa, Shomarka Keita, the late Isaria Kimambo, Paul Lane, Adria La Violette, Jean-Loïc Le Quellec, David Lewis-Williams, Patrick Manning, Bertram Mapunda, Roderick J. McIntosh, Susan Keech McIntosh, the late Joseph C. Miller, Sally Falk Moore, the late Alfred Muzzolini, Catherine Namono, Katharina Neumann, Paul Newman, Derek Nurse, the late Boniface Obichere, the late William Ochieng', the late Atieno Odhiambo, the late Onaiwu Ogbomo, Akinwumi Ogundiran, Gérard Philippson, John Edward Philips, David W. Philipson, Innocent Pikirayi, the late Terence Ranger, Colin Renfrew, Peter Robertshaw, Karim Sadr, the late Romuald Schild, Peter R. Schmidt, the late Thurstan Shaw, Paul Sinclair, Benjamin Smith, Stuart Tyson Smith, Himla Soodyall, the late Taddesse Tamrat, Christian Thibon, Sarah Tishkoff, Marie-Claude Van Grunderbeek, Rainer Vossen, James L. A. Webb, the late Fred Wendorf, Bruce B. Williams, and Edwin N. Wilmsen. I have surely left out many who should be in this list, and to them I sincerely apologize.

From the several generations of PhD students who studied with me at the University of California at Los Angeles I continued to learn more about the discipline of history. Some of these scholars combined written resources with linguistic and comparative ethnographic evidence in their work. Others made critically careful use of oral traditions, joining that kind of evidence with written, linguistic, and comparative cultural evidence, to uncover the cultural, economic, and political histories of particular African societies or regions. Still others foregrounded linguistic historical methods in the reconstruction of *longue durée* regional histories, combining that resource with the available archaeological, oral, and written documentation. These students broadened and deepened my knowledge of history across the continent and my understandings of historical methods. They introduced me to such topics as the history of indigenous medicines and medical beliefs and the roles of religious belief and practice in social and cultural history; and they gave me new awareness of gender and gender relations in African history and new understandings of the historical pathways of political change from small-scale institutions of governance to socially complex states. Many of their names and works receive specific mention in the notes and in the references.

I owe very special thanks to Patrick Manning, the Andrew W. Mellon Professor of World History, Emeritus, of the University of Pittsburgh, to the archaeologist Peter R. Schmidt, and to the biological anthropologist Dr. Shomarka Keita for their invaluable advice and critical feedback that enabled the publication of this book. I am especially grateful to Patrick Manning and Shomarka Keita for their instrumental role in reviewing materials during the final stages of the book's production. This project was also made possible by the skillful work and diligence of Senior History Editor Priya Nelson, Editorial Assistants Barbara Shi and Emma Wagh, Production Editor Theresa Liu, and Copyeditor Beth Gianfagna. My appreciation for their work cannot be overstated.

Last, but very much the opposite of least, I owe a particular debt of gratitude to Henry Louis Gates Jr. for the invitation to give the 2019 Nathan I. Huggins lectures, which led to the writing of this work, and to Abby Wolff, Matthew Weinberg, Velma DuPont, and others on the staff at the Hutchins Center for African and African American Research at Harvard University for making the lectures a rewarding and welcoming experience.

ANCIENT AFRICA

CHAPTER ONE

Introducing the
Issues and Themes

BARELY MORE THAN fifty thousand years ago, the primary
ancestors of every single human being alive today lived in eastern Africa.[1] World history to that point *was* African history.

What seems less generally understood is that, just because
some Africans left the continent around that time, and their
descendants eventually expanded across the rest of the globe,
history did not come to a halt in Africa. Those of our ancestors
who continued to inhabit the common ancestral homelands of
us all, in the eastern parts of Africa, did not fall out of time into
some kind of ahistorical stasis. They, too, expanded their cultures and ways of life into new lands, between fifty thousand and
twenty thousand years ago, spreading westward and southward
out of our common East African homeland regions and establishing themselves across the rest of the continent.

In subsequent ages Africans did not live somewhere off the
edge of the human historical world we all belong to. They participated in and contributed in integral fashion to the developments

that brought into being the world we now all live in. The great transitions of early world history—

the major early technological breakthroughs;
the shift from foraging to agricultural economies;
the emergence of towns—and of states;
the advent of commercial exchange over distance—

all unfolded in Africa during the same broad periods as elsewhere in the world. And these developments took shape across large parts of the continent and not just along its northern fringes.

Moreover, Africa, as the origin land of us all, is the most diverse continent in its human genetics. The peoples of the rest of the world, whose ancestors began spreading outward from Africa fifty thousand or more years ago, form essentially one subset of that African diversity.

And yet the integral intertwining of Africa's past with the overall movements of early world history seems often still not recognized—not because the historical sources and historical information are not there but because of a lack of engagement by too many historians with the full sweep of that body of information and, also, because of sadly persistent and wrong presumptions of the lack of salience of Africa to broader human history before the slave trade. The horrific rationalizations of slavers and slave owners and all the others who benefited from slavery—their appalling, self-justifying myths about Africa as a continent of backward, "uncivilized," and, most horrifically, inherently inferior peoples—live on even today, unexamined in the minds of far too many people around the world. Until we begin to fully integrate Africa into the history we teach everybody, we are not going to finally dispel those baseless assumptions. These are modes of thinking that we continually need to confront and, sooner rather than later, finally and forever eradicate from all our cultural understandings.

So how do we more fully integrate Africa and Africans into our global histories of humankind? How might we organize our history-telling so that each chapter as we move forward in time tells its stories in a fashion that fully accounts for developments in the continent and integrates them into our broader syntheses of history around the globe—so that each chapter of our world history covers a particular broad time span and, at the same time, is truly global in its coverage?

What if we centered our stories on culture and society? What if our focus were on exploring all the variety of ways people around the world, over each succeeding historical age, readapted their lives, activities, social relations, religious beliefs, and material culture—in parallel or in different fashions—to cope with the changing circumstances, natural and cultural, of the world around them? Patrick Manning's new book, *A History of Humanity*, deserves particular attention in this respect.[2] It is a groundbreaking advance in applying those kinds of perspectives to both the very *longue durée* of our common human past and to recent centuries. Telling history in this fashion offers historians new ways for bringing in, as integral actors in the overall human story, not just Africa and Africans, but the peoples of boreal Eurasia, the Americas, the islands of South Asia, and Oceania.

Germane to these issues, I see no value in the artificial separation of our human story into something called "history" and something else called "prehistory." Whatever human beings have done in the past is history. It is not something restricted to places and times with written records. Archaeology and, as we shall see, historical linguistics, together with the long-established historical methods of comparative ethnography, provide powerful tools for revealing the changing material, social, cultural, and religious practices and ideas of peoples of times far back into the past and for establishing the broad chronologies of those histories.

The term "ancient" is used here with the deliberate aim of giving it a global applicability and of extending its chronological scope much farther back in time than the usual applications to such regions of the world as, for example, the Mediterranean and the Middle East. For my purposes here, "ancient" in its broadest sense applies to all the ages from the beginnings of human expansion around the world down to the first three centuries CE, although having particular reference to the periods from the Last Glacial Maximum of a bit more than twenty thousand years ago down to the early first millennium CE. Applying these kinds of perspectives allows me to propose five historical periods from the initial emergence of fully modern humans through the end of the "ancient" era in 300 CE.

68,000 to 20,000 BCE. This initial, long period extends from the emergence in East Africa of the first *fully* modern human communities down through the varied stories of how their descendants spread out across the world. The key initiating development marking the inception of that first age in our story—the defining development that distinguishes the fully modern ancestors of us all from all the other hominin groups— was the creation and adoption for the first time of fully syntactical language. Chapter 6 has more to say about how that uniquely human capacity served as the crucial enabling factor for the spread of humanity around the globe.

The stories of this initiating age spotlight how, in different world regions, the diverse cultural and social ideas and practices of our ancestors took shape and how the communities of those times changed and developed their technologies and food-gathering practices in response to the challenges of the widely differing environments into which they moved. It was the age in which the imagery and symbols of the common early human religion of shamanism came to be expressed, eventually around the world, in rock art. Very early in this age, as well, our human ancestors brought about a major technological advance, namely, the inventions of the first two types of composite projectile weaponry, the bow and arrow and the spear-thrower or atlatl.

Telling these stories would require giving full attention also to the generally neglected but equally important history, during this same long age, of the spread of fully modern humans westward and southward out of the common origin lands of us all in eastern Africa and eventually across the rest of the continent. In Africa, just as in Eurasia, the expansions of our ancestors eventually everywhere replaced their not-quite-fully-modern hominin predecessors. Imparting that history turns out to be its own complex of stories.[3]

20,000–9700 BCE. A new, long, global historical age, characterized by multiple shifts in human adaptations to the world around them, then began from around the height of the Last Glacial Maximum and lasted until the beginning of the Holocene epoch around 9700 BCE. During that period human beings nearly everywhere had to adapt and then readapt their ways of life and their subsistence practices to cope with repeated shifts between cooler and warmer climatic phases, as well as shifts between drier and wetter rainfall regimes.

9700–5000 BCE. A third big thematic period, it can be proposed, extended from the start of the Holocene epoch at around 9700 until around 5500 BCE. Notable climatic fluctuations ushered in the Holocene in most parts of the world. Bringing about major changes in natural environments, these shifts compelled people around the globe to substantially readapt their ways of obtaining food. Most significant of all, people living in as many as eleven or twelve separate and far-flung regions of the world began, independently and stage by stage, to move from hunting and gathering practices to food production—that is to say, from foraging to the deliberate cultivation of crops and raising of livestock. Africans of this era, living in parts of the continent distant from one another, were the independent innovators of at least three of those separate inventions of agricultural ways of life.

6000 to 3000 BCE. A new era, partially overlapping with the age of early agriculture, then took shape from around 6000 to 3000 BCE, a period that we might call the era of agricultural exchange. Sometimes even before 6000 BCE, the inventors of these new ways of subsistence had begun to spread with their agricultural methods into new lands. Because of these early expansions of farming peoples, agricultural systems innovated in one world region eventually began to come into contact with one or more systems innovated in other regions, and those encounters soon led to the diffusion of crops and animals from one system to another.

What gives coherence to this age of agricultural exchange is not the subsistence exchanges alone but the consequences of those processes for social and cultural history. The adoption of new crops and domestic animals enriched the productivity and variety of the agricultural practices of the regions they spread to. In consequence, the proportion of the diet derived from cultivation and herding progressively grew, and the proportion coming from collecting and hunting declined. This increased subsistence productivity enabled agricultural populations to continue to grow—and to grow not just in overall numbers but often in the sizes and densities of the residential groupings and, also in a few regions late in the era, in the size and centralization of the political formations that people belonged to.

3000 BCE to 300 CE. The ensuing period, of the last three millennia BCE and first three centuries CE, was marked by strikingly new developments in society, culture, and economy, along with as the persistence of several earlier historical trends. Notably, as population numbers and density grew in several world regions, larger scales of political organization took shape, with the emergence of kingdoms and, in time, empires. Over the same period, people in several areas of the world gradually readapted their crops and agricultural practices in ways that allowed them to spread their economies into areas with climates previously marginal to farming, such as northern temperate areas of North America and Europe and the rainforest zones of Africa and South America, and also, as in the case of the islands of Oceania, into areas sometimes previously uninhabited by humans.

In addition, from the early second millennium BCE onward, the new developments in technology, along with a growing variety in the goods manufactured by the peoples of different regions, stimulated the rise for the first time of regular trade relations over long distances. By the first millennium BCE the expanding networks of long-distance exchange led, most notably, to the rippling out of the social, cultural, political, and communicational consequences of those developments more and more widely across the African-Eurasian portion of world.

The records of these histories, as already noted, are not just written. They include, for example in the African and Oceanic cases, oral traditions. Historical evidence emerges from the material finds of archaeology; from reconstructing the histories of ancient lexicons of culture, belief, and material life going back to different particular periods in the past;[4] with less precision, from the testimony of comparative ethnography, long used by anthropologists to unveil the ancient roots of more recent cultural practices;[5] and, most effectively, from bringing together the correlative findings of these different approaches. Genetics is a newly important resource, as well, although with interpretive problems of its own, as noted in chapter 5 and in the appendix.

World historians today increasingly do use the findings of archaeology in their works, but the other methods remain mostly unfamiliar. In African historical studies, in contrast, the correlative application of archaeological, historical linguistic, oral traditional, and comparative ethnographic evidence has already a long pedigree, with an extensive body of available work on the relevant methods and their findings.[6]

Through all those periods Africans were essential contributors to the defining trends and developments of human history. Even before the mid-twentieth century, there existed a significant body of evidence on early African history and its wider global connections, provided that one cared to look for it. Up until the 1960s, though, almost the only scholars who did pay such attention to Africa taught at Historically Black Colleges and Universities in the United States. They included not just the well-known William Leo Hansberry at Howard University but professors at other such colleges as well.

But then from the late 1950s and the early 1960s onward, the course of current world events began to change all that. The rise and growing success of independence movements all across Africa, along with the civil rights movement especially in the United States, stimulated a new growth of public and scholarly interest in Africa. Since then, scholarship, especially in the fields of history, historical linguistics, and archaeology, has immensely increased the body of available information on the African past, and courses in African history are now part of the curriculum at many if not most universities and colleges.

But can one say, even yet, that African history is being treated as an *integral* part of the discipline? In the revitalized field of world history, are developments in Africa integral to the overall story, or are they relegated to the add-ons? When African history courses are available at a university, what proportion of undergraduate history majors actually take those courses? And in those courses are teachers giving the same in-depth attention to the ancient periods in Africa that they give to the past few centuries?

So how do we take on these challenges?

First, we need to disseminate a wide historical awareness of what was going on among Africans during the long ages from the beginning of human expansion around the world down to the first three centuries CE. Every student needs to be introduced to human history as it unfolded in Africa in those eras with the same depth of attention and understanding that they currently receive about history elsewhere in the world.

We need to know, and to incorporate integrally into our presentation of world history, the common directionalities and developments that Africa shares with the wider human story of the early ages. To accomplish that, we must convey the facts about technology and invention in ancient Africa, about the export of innovation from the continent in the ancient eras, and about the early rise of African towns and networks of long-distance commercial exchange. These histories have major implications, not just for the integration of Africa into world history, but for our understandings, as readers and writers of history, of our common human past worldwide. And, among other things, these developments have messages for us about the roles, contributions, and place of women in history.

In pursuit of these aims, chapters 2–5 set out some of the notable *longue durée*—that is to say, very long-term—developments that illuminate how history in ancient Africa moved along paths broadly parallel to contemporary courses of change in regions outside the continent; how those developments came to intersect with developments outside the continent; and—equally important— how those developments raise fundamental issues for our understandings of world history more generally. Chapter 2 explores notable cases of technological invention in Africa over the period from the close of the last Ice Age until the first millennium BCE and relates those developments to parallel courses of invention elsewhere in the world. Chapter 3 turns attention to the independent inventions of agricultural ways of life in Africa, taking place broadly over the same periods as the creation of such economies elsewhere in the world. This chapter brings attention, as well, to the spread, beginning in the age of agricultural exchange, of numerous African crops and one key animal, the donkey, to other world regions. Chapter 4 moves on to the seminal contributions of African merchants and tradespeople beginning in the second millennium BCE to the advent and spread of long-distance systems of commerce across the African-Eurasian macrocontinent. Each of these chapters compares changes in Africa with those in other parts of the world, showing the similarities and often the leadership of Africans in innovation.

Chapter 5 turns attention to a different kind of *longue durée* issue—to the task of correcting a view that still appears in many books on world history. This chapter, focusing on the Nile Valley, the Horn of Africa, and the eastern Sahara from earliest times, lays out the deeply African foundations of ancient Egyptian culture, beliefs, and institutions—findings that the archaeological discoveries of the past four decades, backed up by linguistic historical studies, have now made abundantly clear.

More crucially, how do we then incorporate these complexities of ancient African history integrally into our telling of world history? To do so, we need to reshape our interpretive frameworks for understanding ancient world history as a whole. The closing chapter, "Africa and Africans in Early Global History," relying on the same five periods of ancient world history listed above, takes up that task. It does so by proposing an extended rethinking of how we might present the themes of early world history in ways that both fully incorporate Africa and, at the same time, offer integrative perspectives on the human experience around the globe.

Bringing ancient Africa fully into world history does far more than just redress the long-standing neglect and disregard of major, fundamentally important components of our common human story. It not only opens up new vistas into the very long-term global interconnectedness of our world, but it also brings to bear additional bodies of evidence that can expand and deepen our historical knowledge, even for regions where early written documentation exists.

Most of all—as already noted—the long-term courses of history in Africa challenge us to rethink our understandings of how history unfolded in other regions around the globe. Taking this tack shines new light on a range of common assumptions about major connective themes in ancient world history, such as how, when, and where notable early technological transitions actually originated and then spread; when and where the varied transitions from foraging to agriculture took shape in different parts of the world; and when and where long-distance commerce earliest began to link distant regions to each other.

This approach raises questions, as well, for our understandings of ancient social history in different parts of the world; of the evolution of early religious belief systems; of gender and how it played out in the social and political relations of those times; and of the varied ways in which the institutions and organizing beliefs and ideas of early, small-scale human societies were both co-opted and transformed in the emerging complex and stratified societies of the later ancient periods.[7]

From the beginning of the spread, fifty thousand or more years ago, of the fully modern human ancestors of all of us out of eastern Africa—both outward across the world outside Africa and also across the rest of the African continent—the paths of historical change within the continent paralleled and, especially from the early and middle Holocene epoch onward, *integrally fed into* wider global networks of change taking place right across the African-Eurasian macrocontinent. Globalization in its strongest and farthest-reaching forms may be a phenomenon of the recent centuries. But its earliest manifestations and effects go back thousands of years, and the African continent from the beginning fully linked into those wider emerging global trends.

Telling these stories can alert us to a related problem that we tend often not to be aware of, namely, the problem of where we plant our feet. Africa gets treated as peripheral because historians—and, too often, even historians *of* Africa based outside the continent—have not performed the informative and necessary exercise, metaphorically, of planting their feet in the middle of the African continent and looking outward from there at the long-term courses of historical change.[8]

CHAPTER TWO

African Firsts in the History of Technology

AFRICANS LIVING IN the heart of the African continent participated separately and independently in the key technological transitions of ancient world history. And they did so during the same broad eras as peoples in other parts of the globe. In at least two instances, Africans appear to have brought notable technological innovations into being, not only just as early, but even *earlier*, than did people living anywhere else in the world.

As our forebears in Africa and elsewhere took new steps toward greater technological mastery of the world around them, they of course built, as we do today, on the foundations laid by prior advances. Sometimes they put older techniques and processes to new uses. Sometimes they applied older techniques and processes to new kinds of materials.

Two primary, very long-term trendlines of technological descent lead from ancient times down to the more complex technologies of later ages. One line we might characterize as chemical, and the other as mechanical. Each line of development began separately in more than one part of the world, among both Africans and peoples of other continents.

Ceramic Technology in World and African History

The earliest in historical time of these lines of descent in technological innovation took shape with a new development in human mastery of chemical processes—specifically, the *multiple, independent inventions* of ceramic technology in several distantly separated parts of the world. Ceramic technology was a major transitional development in our mastery of the world around us, not only because it is the earliest sophisticated pyrotechnology— that is to say, the earliest formal technology using heat to remake the chemistry and therefore the usefulness of earthen matter—but because of the long-term historical ramifications of that discovery. Ceramic technology was of major significance, initially, because of its contribution to human food preparation and hence its potential effects on human health and human population growth. In the subsequent eras of world *and* African history, ceramic wares often became valued commodities, contributing to the growth of both short- and long-distance commercial enterprise. But what we often may fail to fully appreciate is the foundational place of ceramic technology in the chains of invention that lead down to the technological world of today.

Ceramics in modern-day science are not generally clay-based, as were the original ceramics. Instead, they commonly consist of oxides such as alumina (Al_2O_3) or zirconia (ZrO_2) or of nonoxides such as silicon carbide, among many others. Dental implants, for example, are ceramic, made of alumina and zirconia. Phone chargers use silicide-based ceramic materials. The tiles on space shuttles, which enable them to withstand the great heat of reentry passage through the atmosphere, are also products of silicide ceramic technology.

The very first invention of ceramics did not take place in Africa but rather in East Asia. Recent discoveries place the beginnings of this development at around 18,000 BCE in areas around the

Yangtze valley of China.[1] By around 14,500–12,000 BCE, peoples living across a second set of East Asian lands had begun also to produce pottery, with their earliest known wares found at sites in the Amur River region, more than 1,500 kilometers north of the Yangtze valley,[2] with a subsequent spread of pottery making to Japan. During this period, by the way, because of the lowered ocean levels of the Ice Age, Sakhalin, along with what are today the islands of Japan, formed a peninsula extending south from the lower Amur region of the Asian mainland, one that may at times have also connected to the Asian mainland at the south through Korea. There was no Yellow Sea; instead, land above sea level connected today's Korea to modern-day northern China and areas farther north. In other words, there were no sea barriers to the spread of people or technology across these regions. Not surprisingly, the shared ceramic decoration styles, imitative of basketry patterns, across this set of regions strongly suggest a common origin.[3] Across the wide expanse of lands between the Yangtze and the Amur River regions, however, the earliest pottery yet known is still later in time, so the more northerly East Asian ceramic development seems likely to have been independent of the Yangtze invention of this technology and therefore to have been the second-earliest such invention in world history, rather than the result of a technological diffusion from the south.

But it was Africans who brought into being the *third-earliest* invention of ceramics. Where did that development take place? People living in western Africa—12,000 kilometers distant from the Yangtze region—independently created this technology. By no later than 11,500 years ago, around 9500 BCE, Africans living in what is today the country of Mali were fashioning pottery. The geographical region of this invention lay in the areas south of the great bend of the Niger River (map 2.1).[4] These lands fell within the areas where the proto-Niger-Congo language would have been spoken and thus where the Niger-Congo language family originated.[5] The earliest ceramic inventors of Africa,

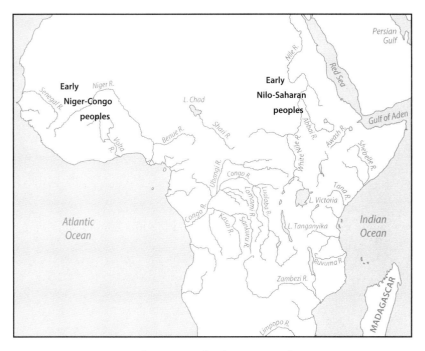

MAP 2.1. Invention of ceramic technology: West Africa, ca. 9500 BCE; eastern Sahara, ca. 8500–8000 BCE.

and third-earliest inventors of ceramic technology in the world, spoke early languages, we believe, of that language family.

What is more, not just the third-earliest, but also the *fourth-earliest* invention of ceramic technology in the world took place in Africa. People living 3,000 kilometers east of Mali, in the southern half of the eastern Sahara, began to fashion ceramic ware almost as early, during the ninth and eighth millennia BCE (see map 2.1).[6] This second African creation of ceramic technology, as our knowledge now stands, is *not* attributable to diffusion from the West African center of invention. Everywhere, this second tradition occurs in regions where people have for millennia spoken, not Niger-Congo languages, but languages of a second major African language family, Nilo-Saharan.[7] And the

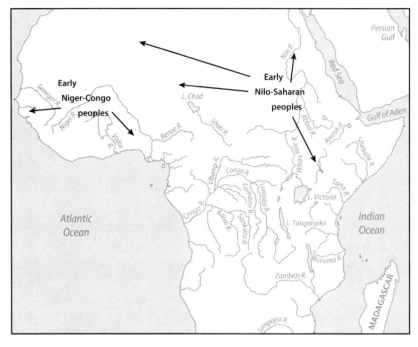

MAP 2.2. Spread of the primary African ceramic inventions,
ca. 8000–6000 BCE.

ceramic wares of this tradition share a common set of decorative
motifs whose arrangements are distinct from those of the earliest pottery of the Niger-Congo-speaking, farther western areas
of the Sudan geographical belt. The overall evidence indicates
that this separate Nilo-Saharan ceramic technology spread from
the east westward into the regions between modern-day Sudan
and Mali (map 2.2).[8]

So Africans living deep in Africa *twice* separately invented
ceramic technology long before—in the case of ancient peoples
in Mali, at least three millennia before—the appearance of
ceramics in the Middle East, and four millennia before this technology began to spread from the Middle East westward to the
eastern parts of Europe.

Women as Inventors and Innovators

The origins of ceramic technology in Africa alert us to something else of historical significance—something of great general importance for historians of early world history everywhere, namely, its gendered aspect.

Women, it appears, were the inventors, the tinkerers, the technological experimenters who created both of the two early African ceramic traditions. The comparative cultural evidence right across the continent strongly supports this inference. Everywhere—except for a very few areas where, in recent centuries, men were able to take over the roles of commercial pottery producers—women have long been the makers of ceramic wares and, often, the guardians not only of the knowledge and practices, but of special rituals meant to ensure the success of their work.[9] Among peoples of the southern savanna belt of Africa, for example, potters were skilled specialists, who viewed their work as a calling.[10] Senior potters who had become mothers carried out ritual observances at deposits of potting clay, affirming their primacy and authority over ceramic manufacture. Women who were menstruating were required to stay away from those sources of clay, as were men and children.

For peoples outside Africa, the past five to six thousand years of patriarchal dominance right through the whole middle belt of the Eurasian landmass have left historians and the general public with the often-unacknowledged presumption of male agency in technological advance. The history of ceramic manufacture in Africa should stand as a great corrective to that presumption, a corrective to how we think about women and men in history.

It tells us that we historians ought to be similarly querying our presumptions about the gender distributions of human agency in all areas of culture and not just in material production. We should be very wary of reading back into pre-urban, pre-state ages the genderings of work and behavior that the intervening several thousand years of unequal and authoritarian societies and cultures brought into being.

Metallurgy in Ancient Africa

But ceramic production was not the only area of early African technological invention. A second major line of early technological advance in ancient world history, fundamental for modern technology, grew out the foundational pyrotechnology of early ceramic production. People in several different parts of the world independently brought metallurgy into existence as a second transformative technology of the ancient eras.

It is surely not accidental that each separate region of the world with early smelting of metals from ores was a region where ceramic technology had previously been established. Possession of ceramic technology meant that people in those regions were already well acquainted with the capacities of fire to change the chemical composition of earthen matter. Metallurgy expanded this understanding of the application of fire to the processing of earthen material, but in a new way. It applied fire and heat not to reshape the chemistry of earthen matter as it was constituted in nature but rather to break that matter down chemically—to separate out parts of such matter and then to form the extracted material into new kinds of cultural items.

As with ceramic technology, the development of metallurgical techniques took place separately in multiple parts of the world. And once again Africans living in the heart of the continent separately initiated this kind of advance. In different parts of the world, copper tended to become the most important of the early metals to be exploited because of its malleability into objects and perhaps for another reason: its melting point, 1,085° C, falls in the same range as the temperatures often generated in the baking of early ceramic wares.[11]

What is actually most arresting about African metallurgical history is the continent's special place in the history of *iron* metallurgy worldwide. In the versions of the histories that used to be taught, and which are commonly still being taught, iron metallurgy had a single beginning in Anatolia around or before the middle second millennium BCE. According to this understanding, within a few centuries this technology began to diffuse outward from that region to the rest of the world, spreading first to the rest of the Levant and the Middle East between 1300 and 1000 BCE and, from there, eastward to India and subsequently also westward toward Europe.

This technology, it was supposed, then passed from southern Arabia across the Red Sea to the Ethiopian Highlands by or before the mid-first millennium BCE. Farther west, in North Africa, the Phoenicians introduced iron at their settlement at Carthage in the late ninth century BCE. Ironworking spread, in addition, by or before the fifth century BCE, to Meroë, either south via Egypt or across the Red Sea from Arabia, with Meroë thereafter becoming a major new iron-producing center (map 2.3).

The conventional assumption used to be that iron then subsequently spread from these introductions along the northern fringe of Africa southward to the rest of the continent. But that view fails in striking fashion to explain the history of ironworking farther south in Africa, south of the Sahara. Already by 1000 to 700 BCE, even *before* the Phoenician settlement at Carthage, ironworking was well established, not only more than 1,500 kilometers farther south in Africa, but at locales extending from east to west across the African savannas. The farthest west of these sites, dating to the eighth or ninth century BCE, were in the lands of the Nok culture of north-central Nigeria. Other sites dating as early have been found in the nearby southwestern Chad basin. And faraway to the east, in Rwanda, the archaeologist Marie-Claude Van Grunderbeek and her team excavated smelting furnaces dating to as early as the mid-eighth century BCE (fig. 2.1).[12] Africans living well south into the African continent, as this chronological evidence shows conclusively, must have independently invented ironworking.

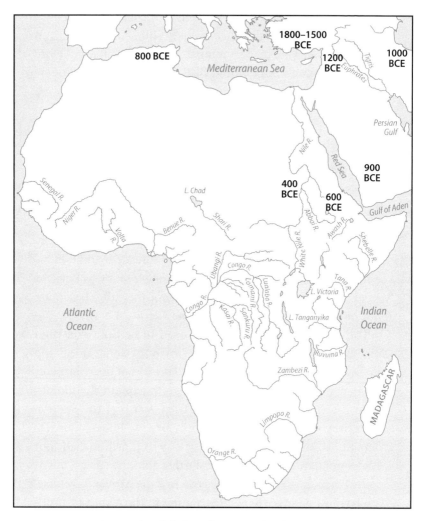

MAP 2.3. Conventional dating of centers of early iron technology.

The distribution of these early iron-smelting sites leads to two further salient expectations. First, this geographical spread makes it highly probable that the lands of the African originators of ironworking lay somewhere in the 1,500 kilometers of woodland savanna stretching between central Nigeria and the

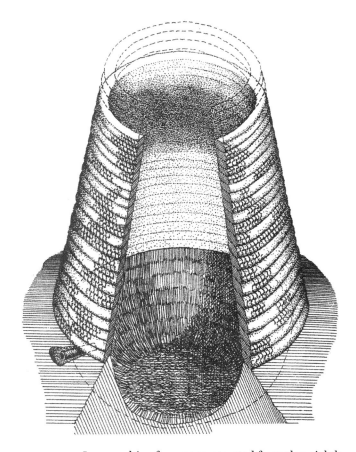

FIGURE 2.1. Iron-smelting furnace constructed from clay, eighth century BCE, Rwanda.

farthest northwestern fringe of East Africa (arrows on maps 2.4 and 2.5). And, second, the vast spread of these sites that had already occurred by nearly three thousand years ago indicates that the foundational earlier sites are likely to date centuries before 1000 BCE. In the past two decades two new archaeological finds of even earlier Africa ironworking have come to light. Not at all surprisingly, their locations and dates fit in with these expectations as to the likeliest areas of African ironworking invention. The two sites—Ôboui, located in the western Central African

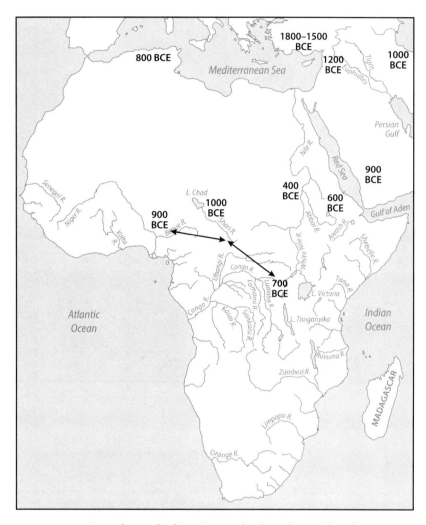

MAP 2.4. Sites of central African iron technology that predate theories of its spread from elsewhere.

Republic, and Gbatoro, located just 100 kilometers across the border in present-day Cameroon—can be dated by radiocarbon to 1800 BCE or earlier (map 2.5).[13]

The published reports show these to have been excavations carried out with care and thoroughness. The sites were undisturbed, sealed above and below by well-defined layers. The assemblies of

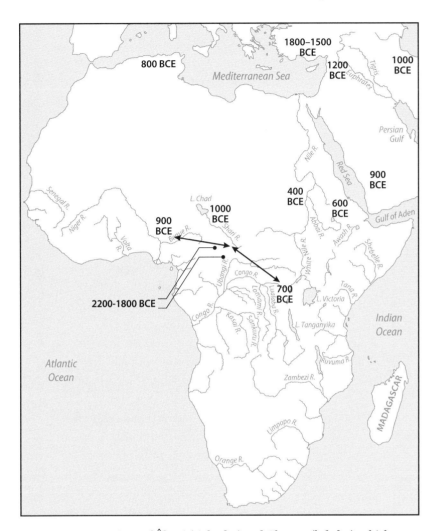

MAP 2.5. Locations of Ôboui (right dot) and Gbatoro (left dot), which provide evidence of African iron technology by at least 1800 BCE.

ironworking materials in each site are extensive. At Ôboui, all the steps in the smelting and forging of iron—all of what archaeologists call the *chaîne opératoire*—are represented in materials from the excavated workshop: furnace structures, tuyeres, iron bits, slag, and stone anvils for hammering the iron, along with large quantities of datable charcoal. These sites, of around four thousand years ago, represent the earliest ironworking yet known, not just in Africa, but anywhere in the world. They are not just too early in time, but separated by far too great a geographical distance, to allow for any possible outside-of-Africa source for the technology.

By no later than 1000–800 BCE the knowledge and methods of iron-smelting had reached as far east across today's Central African Republic as the communities speaking languages of the Central Sudanic branch of the Nilo-Saharan family, who resided in the lands around the western borders of modern-day South Sudan. Detailed mapping of the spread of the terminologies not just for iron and the forging process, but for early iron tools and implements, reveals that this technology spread in the very early first millennium BCE from the Central Sudanic-speaking peoples, both eastward to the ancestral Nilotic-speaking societies of South Sudan and southward to the Bantu peoples newly arriving during this period at the northwestern edges of East Africa.[14]

The spread of words relating to iron and ironworking from the Central Sudanic peoples to the ancestors of such modern-day Nilotic peoples as the Bari, Nuer, and Dinka of South Sudan— among them, a word for the smith's anvil (*-kun-) and two terms for the bellows for heating the forge (*ngbuk- and *ok-/*uk-)[15]— make it clear that this technology reached South Sudan from the Central African Republic to the west, and *not* from Meroë to the north. Interestingly, though, in the west of South Sudan this eastward diffusion of words for iron and iron technology finally reached its limit. There, along the borders with modern-day Ethiopia, this eastward spread of these words (straight arrows on map 2.6) came up against a countervailing spread southward from the northern Ethiopian Highlands of a separate body of ironworking terms (curving arrows on map 2.6).[16] Apparently, it was in eastern South Sudan that the spread of the separate inventions of iron metallurgy, eastward from central Africa and southward from the Middle East, met up, probably around the middle of the first millennium BCE.

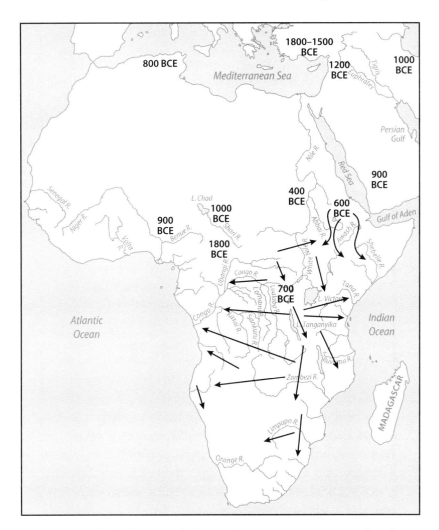

MAP 2.6. The further spread of iron technology to eastern, central, and southern Africa as revealed by the diffusion of lexicons of ironworking.

Farther south, along the great Western Rift zone of Africa, the key early terms relating to iron and iron technology among the earliest Mashariki Bantu of the early first millennium BCE— ancient words for iron ore, for the bellows used in smelting furnaces, and for the smith's hammer for hammering iron, as well

Table 2.1. Iron Terms Borrowed from Central Sudanic into Bantu Languages

Iron-related words borrowed in the first millennium BCE into proto-Mashariki (Narrow Eastern) Bantu from Central Sudanic languages	
*-òndò, *-ùndò "smith's hammer"	Central Sudanic *ɔndɔ "to forge (iron)"
*-bu̱lu / *-bulu / *bulo- "iron; iron ore"	Central Sudanic: Beli 6ulo "iron"
*-kumbi "iron hoe"	Central Sudanic: Moru-Madi *(k)ombi
*-kúngù, *-gúngù "iron hoe"	Central Sudanic: Moru-Madi *kongo
*-èlé "iron knife"	Central Sudanic *ele "blade, knife"
Ironworking term borrowed into the northwestern rainforest Bantu languages spoken westward from the areas in which the proto-Mashariki language was spoken	
*-kuka "bellows"	Central Sudanic: Moru-Madi *(k)oka "bellows"

as for iron hoes and iron knives—similarly came from the Central Sudanic languages spoken in the areas where today's territories of the Central African Republic, South Sudan, Congo, and Uganda conjoin.[17] These words (table 2.1) reveal the diffusion southward of iron and associated new implements and productive activities from those regions to the early Mashariki Bantu, who around the beginning of the first millennium BCE would have been advancing from the west into the areas along Africa's great Western Rift, immediately south of the Central Sudanic-speaking regions. The lands of the early Mashariki speakers would have extended in those times from Rwanda in the north, where Van Grunderbeek and her team located smelting furnaces dating as early as the eighth century BCE, southward through the 1,000-kilometer stretch of lands along

Lake Tanganyika. (The arrow on map 2.6 pointing to "700 BCE" marks the initial stage of this spread of ironworking, to the early Great Lakes Bantu.)

The subsequent expansions of Mashariki Bantu-speaking communities at the close of the first millennium BCE and the very beginning of the first millennium CE then carried iron-working far across eastern and southeastern Africa. (The arrows on map 2.6 pointing east and south from the Great Lakes track this historical stage.) From no later than the middle of the first millennium BCE, iron, iron technology, and the fashioning of iron implements also began a further spread westward from the African Great Lakes region, across Bantu-speaking central Africa, from the Western Rift region to the Atlantic Ocean. The mapping of the extensive body of lexical evidence bearing on this history shows that this technology passed westward from the earliest Mashariki Bantu communities via three main lines of spread toward the Atlantic (westward-pointing arrows on map 2.6):[18]

> through the equatorial rainforest along and north of the
> middle Congo River;[19]
> along the Sankuru River region at the southern edges
> of the rainforest;
> and through the savanna belt south of the rainforest.

The first of these spreads of iron, through the northern parts of the rainforest, met up west of the Ubangi-Congo confluence with a countervailing spread south of iron from Cameroon and the western parts of the Central African Republic.

Yet there is still another remarkable African first in iron technology that we must take into account. As the investigations by the archaeologist Peter Schmidt have revealed, by the end of the first millennium BCE, African iron smelters living in the African Great Lakes region began to construct furnaces capable of generating sufficiently high temperatures to produce carbon steel directly from the smelt. And this is no small matter. Europeans did not learn to produce steel by a single step until the invention—*two thousand years later*, in the nineteenth century—of the Bessemer process.[20] The Chinese were also ahead of the West in this respect. They had developed capacities for directly producing steel by the eleventh century CE. But even their advance took place centuries after African smelters already had attained this capability.[21]

Iron produced in many parts of Africa for a long time remained superior in quality to unforged, raw iron from Europe. West Africans were well aware of the excellence of their iron, as we see in their responses to the availability of iron coming from Europe in the fifteenth to eighteenth centuries CE. Not only did Africans prefer the product of their own smelters and smiths in actual toolmaking, but the Portuguese, for example, who dominated the coastal trade in the sixteenth and seventeenth centuries, bought higher-quality iron from African producers in today's Sierra Leone and Liberia and transported it around the coast to Guinea and Senegal to exchange for other products, notably gold, leather, and—beyond regrettably—human beings.

This history raises two other questions for our consideration.

First, just how might Africans in the far western Central African Republic and the adjacent parts of Cameroon have come to discover iron four thousand or more years ago, and how to extract it? We know the usual story: that metallurgical technology began with metals with lower melting points than iron and with metals that, like copper, might occur not just hidden in ores, but as impure bits of metal imbedded but visible in them. Only after working with easier-to-extract metals would people have been able to conceive of the possibility that—by applying more intense temperatures—there might be other kinds of metals to be extracted from ores.

But in large parts of the African continent, and specifically in what now appears to be the earliest ironworking locations—not just in the Central African Republic, but nearly everywhere south of the Sahara—the knowledge and use of iron *preceded* the use of copper. So having a prior knowledge of copper smelting does not seem to be the explanatory factor for Africa.

Again, ceramic technology may be implicated in explaining this history. Widely in Africa, potters fire their ceramics in pits dug into the earth. And that brings our attention to an interesting additional factor. A great many areas in the woodland savanna belt extending from West Africa to the eastern edges of the Central African Republic have lateritic soils with very high iron oxide content. The archaeologist Merrick Posnansky and others have proposed that pottery firing at higher temperatures led to the incidental production, probably on repeated occasions, of bits of iron from the high-iron lateritic soil. And in that way iron would have come to the attention of people in that region.

At this point gender once again enters into the story. Men rather than women were apparently the ones who first began to find uses for this new kind of material, a by-product of women's technology. Everywhere across Africa it was men who took up smelting and who developed the rituals and symbols that validated a gendered distribution of labor in the working of iron. Nevertheless, women widely continued to have roles in the new technology, often as the miners of iron ore and, in southern Africa and probably elsewhere, applying their ceramic skills to such tasks as fashioning the ceramic tuyeres carrying oxygen from the bellows into the smelting furnaces and also the crucibles used particularly in the processing of a different metal, copper.[22]

Historical Connections of Copper to Iron Metallurgy in Africa

But what of the history of copper and iron in farther northern parts of Africa? In those regions the history of metallurgy accorded with the more usual expectations of historians, with copper as the first metal of major importance; with ironworking not spreading to those areas until the first millennium BCE; and with both technologies coming from the Levant. Copper technology appears to have reached the Egyptian corner of the African continent initially in the fourth millennium BCE, in the form of native copper extracted from deposits in the Sinai Peninsula. Used initially to fashion decorative items, it eventually became an important metal for practical use as Egypt moved fully into the Bronze Age in the early third millennium.

Only slightly later—in the middle third millennium BCE— 2,500 kilometers away from Egypt, in the Aïr Mountain Range of today's country of Niger, another African people, most probably speakers of a Nilo-Saharan language belonging to the western sub-branch of the Sahelian branch of that family,[23] initiated their own separate development of copper metallurgy. The archaeologist Augustin Holl has argued that the earliest sites in Aïr with copper, dating from 2500 to 1500 BCE, reveal a period of experimentation with different furnace configurations for smelting copper ores. By no later than 1500 BCE the smelters of this region had settled on a particular furnace type and brought into being a mature copper smelting technology.[24] From the producing areas in the Aïr Range, copper soon began to be traded widely southward and westward in West Africa. Linguistic evidence developed by the historian Constanze Weise indicates that trade in copper had reached southwestward from Aïr to the northwestern parts of modern-day Nigeria sometime before 1000 BCE.[25] Soon after, no later than the ninth century BCE, the technology of copper smelting had spread a thousand kilometers farther west, to present-day southern Mauritania.[26]

For more recent eras we know of one other notable copper-producing area in the Sahel latitudes of Africa, far to the east in the Darfur region. During the second millennium CE it was an important source of copper for a wide expanse of regions far to its south, as far as today's northeastern Congo. Might this have been also a very early region of African copper production? We simply do not currently know, because the whole set of regions in and around Darfur, despite their undoubted historical importance, are so far almost entirely unexplored archaeologically.

But, strikingly, everywhere farther south in Africa the establishment of iron metallurgy clearly preceded the utilization of copper. Across two-thirds of the continent it was the prior possession of iron technology, it seems, that led people to the discovery and the smelting of copper ores. The most notable such region of invention comprised today's "Copper Belt," a stretch of copper-rich lands extending from central Zambia into the southern Democratic Republic of Congo. People speaking a Bantu language of the Sabi subgroup began exploiting the local ores no later than around the fourth century CE,[27] several centuries after the spread of iron technology across those areas. This region soon became the source, via community-to-community trade, of the spread of copper and copper items all across the Zambezi River watershed, as well as along the rivers leading northward into the Congo basin. A new set of Bantu communities spread across the region from around the eighth century, with their language, ancestral to the modern-day Luba dialects of those areas, progressively displacing the earlier Sabi language from use, and with the production, trade, and demand for copper all the while continuing to grow.[28]

A second notable area of probable independent discovery and exploitation of copper resources lay in areas along the north side of the Congo River, just inland from the Atlantic Ocean. The local artisans of this area brought copper metallurgy into being at an as-yet-unknown time, possibly not until the later first millennium CE but, in any case, centuries after the arrival of iron technology there. Control of the trade in copper from these sources became a major factor in the founding and rise to power of the Kingdom of Kongo in the fourteenth and fifteenth centuries.

Mechanical Invention in Early World and African History

The second important technological trajectory—mechanical rather than chemical in nature—descended as well from ancient forms of production to strategies still employed today. My particular focus in this case is the loom weaving of textiles. Textile producers nowadays rely on machine looms and mass production rather than on individual weavers, and they fashion textiles out of a variety of new kinds of later invented materials. But the methods of later ages and of modern times evolved out of developments that began as early as the middle of the Holocene epoch.

In the global context cotton textiles stand out as having particularly wide early historical importance. What is especially noteworthy is that people independently invented the weaving of cotton textiles in at least three, and possibly four, separate parts of world. The multiple origins of particular technologies in world history is something we have already encountered in considering the histories of ceramics and metallurgy: that peoples living far apart in distant regions of the world independently set out on parallel trajectories of technological innovation and that they set in motion these histories of invention thousands of years ago.

In keeping with the several independent origins of cotton textile production, the inventors in each region of invention domesticated a different species of cotton indigenous to their region:

> in the Americas, two species: one in Peru, *Gossypium barbadense*, and a separate species in Central America and Mexico, *Gossypium hirsutum*;
> and in India and Africa, two species have been documented across a wide region, *Gossypium herbaceum* and *Gossypium arboretum*.[29]

So, which of these parallel developments was the earliest?

We have in this case, it appears, still another African first. The earliest evidence of the processing of cotton in the world

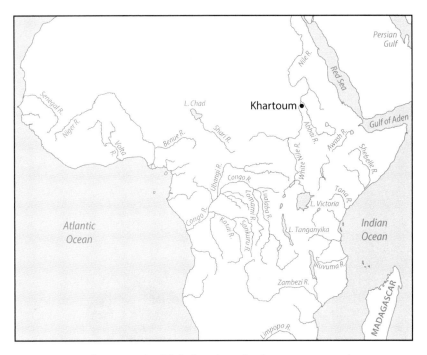

MAP 2.7. Khartoum site, likely location of early cotton processing,
sixth millennium BCE.

comes from today's country of Sudan, although the evidence
thus far is indirect rather than direct. The finds consist not yet
of cotton textile fragments, but rather of the spindle whorls used
for spinning cotton thread. These spindle whorls occur in sites
of the Khartoum culture of Sudan (map 2.7), with a calibrated
dating of the sixth millennium BCE.[30] Figure 2.2 presents two
examples of these items, each having the classic flat, round shape
typical of African versions of this item, and contrasts them with
a quite differently shaped item from the Khartoum site, which
may indeed have been a fishing weight.[31] This evidence dates
about a thousand years before the earliest Indian cotton that
has been dated with certainty, and a thousand to two thousand
years before the earliest American cotton, in Peru.

FIGURE 2.2. Spindle whorls from the Khartoum Neolithic. The two flat, round items on the right could have been used for spinning cotton thread, whereas the one on the left might have been a fishing weight.

The added fact that these spindle whorls were ceramic items exemplifies an accompanying phenomenon that commonly occurs in history—of people applying techniques from one kind of technology to another. In this case weavers reapplied the existing Sudanic ceramic technology for fashioning pots to the fashioning of a new kind of item, the spindle whorl.

From the eastern parts of the Sudan belt, cotton textile making had spread to West Africa by no later than probably the second millennium BCE. Cotton textile weavers in most of West Africa wove their cotton cloth in long strips on horizontal looms.

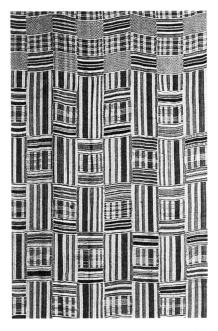

FIGURE 2.3. Modern-day kente cloth.

The weavers then sewed together the resulting narrow lengths of cloth to make the garment, a technique that has become a lasting tradition. Kente cloth from modern-day Ghana is a particularly well-known example (fig. 2.3).[32]

But that is not all there is to tell about this kind of mechanical invention in Africa. A second, independent African invention of loom production of textiles took place in West Africa. Far from Sudan, Africans who would have spoken early languages of the South Volta-Congo branch of the Niger-Congo family brought into being their own separate invention of loom weaving, producing raffia fabrics (fig. 2.4). The origin lands of raffia weaving lay in the rainforest extending across today's southern Nigeria and into Cameroon, lands where the raffia palm is a native tree. Archaeological investigations of this technology have been few as yet. But the distributional and ethnographic

FIGURE 2.4. Raffia cloth from the Kuba people of Central Africa.

evidence requires that the origins of this technology go back to at least the fourth millennium BCE.

Early Bantu-speaking communities, from around 3000 BCE onward, took this technology along with them as they expanded southward deep into and through the equatorial rainforest regions. By the close of the first millennium BCE, their descendants had carried this technology as far south as the forest-savanna mosaic areas of the Lower Congo River areas and as far east as the far western edge of eastern Africa.

The inventors of raffia cloth technology devised a quite different, upright broadloom to carry out their weaving, and that kind of loom spread wherever their descendants took this technology. And because of this prior history, when the knowledge of cotton textile weaving eventually diffused to peoples of today's southern Nigeria, the local textile weavers often adapted their existing broadloom to the weaving of cloth from the new source of textile fiber. For centuries raffia cloth remained a highly valued item of social as well as economic and commercial importance, both in the areas inland from the coasts of the Bight of Biafra and all across central Africa. In some areas of western central Africa people began centuries ago to produce standard sizes of raffia cloth to serve specifically as currency, in other words, money—just how many centuries ago we do not yet know, but possibly quite early.

Issues and Propositions

There are at least three sets of lessons to draw here.

First—as to ceramics—the third *and* fourth earliest inventions of this technology in all of world history took place in two far-separated regions in Africa. Just as notably, African women appear to have brought this technology into being, and they did so several thousand years before the adoption of ceramic technology in the usual regions that people think of as early "civilizations," such as the Levant and Egypt.

Second, in the case of ironworking, the earliest dated sites in the world for the smelting of iron, going back four thousand or possibly more years, are located in the Central African Republic and neighboring parts of Cameroon, in the middle of the continent. The inventors of this technology lived in small-scale communities and not in some kind of stratified, centralized society. And we should note one other point about African metallurgical inventiveness: African smelters were the first, centuries before anyone else, to develop furnaces able to generate sufficient heat for single-step production of steel.

A third lesson concerns the loom weaving of cotton textiles. From the artifactual evidence, the earliest people in the world to bring this particular kind of technology into being would have been Nilo-Saharan-speaking Africans living in Sudan in the sixth millennium BCE. As I show in chapter 4, this technology spread by or before the second millennium BCE as far west as the savanna belt of West Africa.

Meanwhile, no later than the fourth millennium BCE and apparently quite independently, Africans living in the forested lands around today's southern Nigeria—speakers of languages of the Niger-Congo language family—invented their own kind of loom technology. Their product was a different kind of cloth, woven from the leaf fibers of the indigenous raffia palm of those areas. Early Bantu-speaking peoples then took this technology with them as they spread south into the wide Congo basin and beyond over the last three thousand years BCE.

In sum, developments in Africa—and, as I consider further in chapter 3, not just in technology—moved ahead along similar historical vectors during the same broad ages as among the peoples of other continents. It is far past time that the discipline of history should take account of this fact. It is far past time that the discipline ceases to treat Africa as something exotic or peripheral and instead begins to bring the complex and varied histories of that continent integrally into the overall story of humankind.

CHAPTER THREE

Ancient Africa and the Export of Agricultural Innovation

AFRICANS SOUTH OF the Sahara, as we have seen, did not live somewhere off the edge of the human historical world we all belong to. They participated in and contributed in integral fashion to the great transitions of world history—to the developments that brought into being the world we now all live in. They were also integral participants in the early global interchanges of world history. Contravening long-held conventional presumptions, the African continent in the ancient eras was very much *a net exporter* of new things to other parts of the world. Once again, the core source regions of these contributions—as was true of the African contributions to technological advance in ancient world history—lay, not on the peripheries of Africa, but in the heart of the continent.

In Africa, as in other parts of the globe, the common initiating factor in the long history of cultural change that leads down to our modern world was the slow and uneven shift, across a period of many centuries, from the old foraging, food-collecting economies of humanity to a new kind of subsistence—one based on the deliberate tending and raising of crops and animals for food, although normally along with the continued use of the older, wild kinds of food resources as well.

The Era of Early Agriculture

The Age of Agricultural Beginnings had multiple origins. People in twelve or more geographically separated, far-flung regions of the world independently set these developments in motion, twelve thousand to seven thousand years ago, in the early Holocene— in the so-called Fertile Crescent; in West Africa; in the eastern Sahara and Sahel of Africa; in the southern Ethiopian Highlands; in northern China; in southern China; in highland New Guinea; in highland South America; in lowland northeastern South America; in Mesoamerica; in India, possibly in three separate regions of the subcontinent;[1] and, by around seven thousand years ago, in what is today the eastern central parts of the United States (the "Eastern Agricultural Complex").[2]

In each region of origin, agriculture began with people's first deliberate cultivation of one or more of the plant foods that they had previously gathered from the wild and, in some areas, with the first tending and protecting of one or two animals that they had formerly hunted. These histories each passed through several initiatory stages.

Communities that, for example, had previously harvested wild grain for food might initiate the shift toward agriculture by beginning each year to keep a portion of the harvested wild grain in reserve. With the arrival of the next rainy season, they could then clear small fields and sow them with the grain seeds that they had reserved from the previous harvest. To increase productivity further they would soon have discovered that they needed to remove competing weeds from the fields and, as the grain crop began to mature, also needed to take such measures as sending the children of the community to the fields to drive away birds and small mammals that might eat the ripening grain.

In the case of early herding of livestock, archaeological finds of the eighth millennium BCE from such sites as Nabta Playa and Bir Kiseiba in the eastern Sahara suggest that one tactic useful in initiating the protection of wild cattle in this region may have been the digging of wells and waterholes near homesteads to attract cattle in the dry season. As cattle became comfortable with a close human presence, local communities could then initiate other activities leading over the long term toward domestication, such as driving the animals out to pasture in the day and herding them into pens in the evening to protect them from predators.

In each of the various world regions of agricultural origins, both the activities of cultivation and the preferences of farmers began to bring about genetic alterations in the crops people raised, gradually changing those crops from their wild into their domesticated versions. This kind of development was, however, slow and incremental; typically, one thousand or even three thousand years might pass after cultivation was begun before demonstrably domesticated versions of an originally wild crop become identifiable in the archaeological record. Similarly, the herding and protecting of originally wild animals only gradually, over many centuries, bred into them the full characteristics of the domesticated livestock species we know from later times.

This new stage in economic history in each case soon had a major demographic consequence. The deliberate cultivation of particular plants as food sources meant that people could produce far more food on the same amount of land than they could by foraging alone and do so close to home. A community could now support an ongoing growth in population simply by bringing successively more land under cultivation. Customs commonly practiced among hunter-gatherer societies, both recently and in ages long past, that would have kept down population growth—notably, continuing to breastfeed children until three and four years of age[3]—would no longer have been needed.

It should be noted that some scholars suggest a different explanation for population growth—that a lessened workload for women eventually came about with agriculture, with the lessened work pressures enhancing their ability to conceive.[4] But this idea seems to show a rather sexist lack of understanding of just how demanding women's lives continued to be down to the present in most parts of the rural world. My own field experience suggests quite the opposite—that women in societies that still today subsist by gathering and hunting tend to carry out their work in more leisurely fashion than do farming women. In contrast, among Niger-Congo-speaking farming societies, spread across almost half of Africa, women are not only the keepers of the household and the food preparers for the whole family, but they carry out as well the great majority of the actual farm labor, from planting to weeding to harvesting. This kind of life experience is hardly unique to women in Africa.

In any case, as societies more and more came to utilize cultivated foods for their sustenance, they could, and did, grow in size. As their populations grew in numbers, they began to expand successively outward from their areas of origin, into new lands. Most often, but not always, the expanding farmers soon outcompeted the existing foraging communities for resources because of their larger community sizes and the greater productivity of their subsistence. The swamping of the earlier hunter-gatherer populations of Europe by the advance westward of farmers in the seventh and sixth millennia from the Middle East provides a striking example.[5]

In a few regions of the world, the foraging populations adopted the raising of crops or animals from nearby farming populations and, having done so, successfully set in motion their own transitions from food collection to food production. Egypt and North Africa of around the seventh and sixth millennia BCE are notable instances. In this period several crops, notably wheat and barley, domesticated in the Levant, along with livestock raising, spread by diffusion to the peoples of those regions, who then integrated the new food resources into their existing economies and cultures. The archaeology shows that overall cultural continuity persisted across this transition—that this development took place in both Egypt and throughout North Africa without a significant influx of any new populations.[6] The new crops fit in well with the long-established, productive reliance on wild grain harvesting in both regions; and the narrow and arid geographical bottleneck of the intervening Sinai region would have hindered rather than encouraged any major accompanying population movements.

In some regions a different kind of obstacle, the need to adapt crops to a different climatic regime, also slowed the advance of agriculture sufficiently for foraging people ahead of the encroaching agricultural frontier to have time to adapt to the challenge. Algonkian-speaking peoples of New England, the upper Middle West, and southern Canada provide a particularly notable set of examples. The longer, colder winters, along with the wide occurrence of rocky, uninviting soils in New England and parts of the Great Lakes region, limited the areas that, respectively, the ancestral Iroquois and Siouan speakers, with their crops coming from the warmer regions to the south, could initially succeed in taking over. And those limitations allowed the Algonkians over the past two millennia gradually to add the cultivation of crops, such as squash, beans, and maize, to the previously existing hunting and gathering components of their subsistence.

In like manner, the boreal forest zone of eastern Europe apparently also proved initially inhospitable to the spread of agriculture northward. The constraints of environment, it can be argued, allowed the early speakers of languages of the Uralic language family, whose lands, around the fifth and fourth millennia BCE, would have lain in those boreal regions, to gradually incorporate elements of food production into their economies. With the new productive capacities, they then began their own expansions, spreading different combinations of foraging and farming and foraging and herding widely northward, as far in some cases as the Arctic coastlands.

Similarly, the spread of livestock raising around two thousand years ago to Khoesan-speaking peoples living in the dry lands of central and western southern Africa—lands marginal for crop cultivation—allowed these communities to develop their own pastoral way of life and spread their culture and economy over large parts of those regions. A still different example is provided by the Okiek peoples of Kenya, who preserved their separate foraging economies down to recent centuries, simply because they lived in the high, colder, forested environments poorly suited to the cultivation of tropical African crops. The Batwa (the so-called Pygmies) of the equatorial rainforest adapted in yet another fashion to the arrival, in their case, of Bantu-speaking farmers from around 3000 BCE onward, by taking on the role of specialized producers of forest products, which for many centuries they traded to their agricultural neighbors in exchange for cultivated foods and other goods.[7]

But more generally in world history the new arrivals with their agricultural practices soon displaced or marginalized the foraging societies, eventually, sometimes centuries later, assimilating of the remnants of the earlier inhabitants into their farming communities.

African Agricultural Beginnings

So how did the early agricultural age play out in Africa? Over the course of the first half of the Holocene epoch, Africa was, as just noted above, home to three different regions of the independent or largely independent invention of agricultural ways of life. One of these was in West Africa, with its formative developments taking place in the period from the tenth to the sixth millennia BCE. The builders of this tradition spoke languages of the Niger-Congo language family.[8]

Far to the east, the southern and middle parts of the farther eastern Sahara formed a second seminal region of agricultural innovation during the first half of the Holocene. Two different sets of peoples contributed to these developments. In areas around and extending westward from the Nile, the primary actors spoke early languages of the Nilo-Saharan family. In the adjacent lands east of the Nile and along the Red Sea Hills region, the peoples who shared in these developments spoke very early languages of the Cushitic branch of the Afrasian (also known as "Afroasiatic") language family.[9] The numerous linguistic descendants of the proto-Cushitic-speaking people include societies that many people will recognize.[10] One example are the Bedauye—more commonly called by the Arabic version, Beja, of their self-name—who today occupy the middle and southern parts of the African Red Sea Hills region. The Cushitic-speaking people perhaps best-known to Western audiences, though, are the Soomaali, whose lands lie farther south in the Horn of Africa.[11]

The third region of agricultural origins in Africa lay in the far southwestern parts of the Ethiopian Highlands. The instigators of farming in this region spoke languages of a different branch of the Afrasian family, the Omotic branch. The Omotic-speaking peoples created a rather different agricultural system, based on the cultivation of Ethiopian yams and the enset plant, the corm and inner stalk of which still provide the staple of the diets of a wide variety of peoples across the southern Ethiopian regions today.[12]

The evidence bearing on the early histories of these several African agricultural systems have been examined in a variety of publications.[13] My approach here is to focus on a compact version of just one of these histories in order to show two things:

how ancient word histories serve as historical documents of the past; and

how even our current, very uneven African archaeological information, with all its gaps, allows us to propose broad, provisional time scales of agricultural developments.

Early Agriculture in West Africa

In the previous chapter I considered, among other topics, the third-earliest invention of ceramic technology, which took place in Mali in the tenth millennium BCE. This development, as it turns out, was part and parcel of an overall transformative shift in culture and economy among the Niger-Congo-speaking peoples of that region, initially to the intensive collecting of wild grains and then, over the next two or three millennia, to the first cultivation of those grains. These successive shifts were, as well, tied into a major climatic development—specifically, the end of the Younger Dryas period, the last phase of the most recent Ice Age. In other words, just as well as elsewhere in the world, so also in Africa, the climatic shifts at the close of the last Ice Age seem to have been driving factors in the various independent developments of agriculture.

In the African case, when the Younger Dryas period came to an end and the Holocene epoch began, around 9700 BCE, rainfall increased across most of the continent. As that happened, a rapid spread northward of savanna grasslands took place in today's central Mali, into what had been previously the southern fringes of an intensely arid Sahara.

As people followed the northward expansion of grassland, they began to use this environment to create a new kind of subsistence economy. They began to collect wild grains as the new staples of their diet. The archaeologists and archaeobotanists who have extensively investigated the sites of this cultural changeover have shown that these people—makers of the Ounjougou culture—cooked their grains whole. What allowed them to do so was their contemporaneous invention of ceramic technology. With that technology they fashioned the pots for cooking their new kind of staple food.[14]

The Ounjougou sites are situated in the heart of the stretch of lands in which the ancestral Niger-Congo language (proto-Niger-Congo) would have been spoken. As the locations of all the

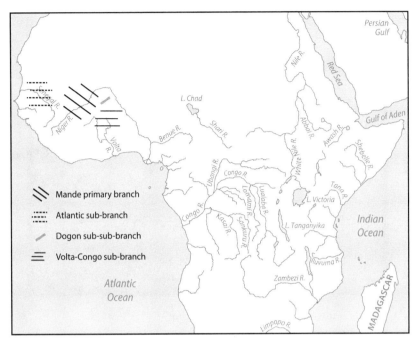

MAP 3.1. Early locations of Niger-Congo speakers, ca. 9000–6000 BCE.

deepest branches of the family reveal (map 3.1), the first several periods in the divergence of that language family spread Niger-Congo speakers west and east across the savannas from modern-day Senegal in the west through Mali and Burkina Faso to the westernmost edges of Nigeria. (See figure 3.2 for the family tree of these early branches.) In those lands in which the earliest stages of divergence and expansion of the Niger-Congo family took place, the archaeology of the early and middle Holocene belongs to what has been called the West African Microlithic tradition. The tool kit of the Ounjougou culture of the innovators of Africa's earliest ceramic technology was an early version of that toolmaking tradition.

A major new period of the expansion of Niger-Congo speakers began in the sixth millennium BCE. In that period

FIGURE 3.1. Stone ax and adz from West African sites.

the speakers of the ancestral language of a particular sub-sub-branch of the family—South Volta-Congo—opened up a new front of settlement. They moved from the more open savannas of the western Sudan belt, southward and southeastward into higher-rainfall woodland savanna and rainforest environments. For this era historians have a new specific archaeological dating correlation to work with: we can give a rough dating of the sixth millennium BCE to the arrival and spread of South Volta-Congo peoples across these regions. Specifically, the areas occupied by the first era of the spread of South Volta-Congo languages correlate closely on the map with the areas of a parallel archaeological spread dating to that time—the spread of newly invented tools: stone axes and adzes (fig. 3.1; map 3.2). The comparative ethnographic, as well as lexical, evidence indicates that the ax in particular—a tool used in clearing woodland and forest land for settlement and cultivation—may originally also have had a second

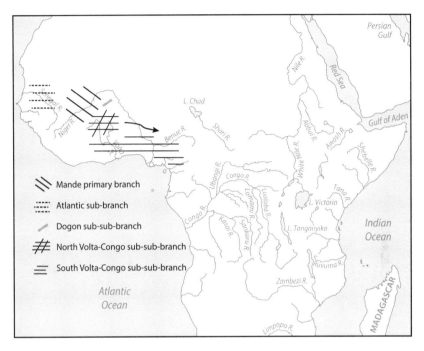

MAP 3.2. Locations of polished stone ax cultures and
South Volta-Congo speakers, 5000–3000 BCE.

important use: to make thin slices into fragile forest soils, into
which the farmer would insert yam cuttings for cultivation.[15]

Setting out the family tree of Niger-Congo language descent
(fig. 3.2) allows us to track the word histories that reveal the
growing shift toward the cultivation of crops over the period
from the Ounjougou culture down to the early South Volta-
Congo era.[16] To the earliest stage of Niger-Congo history, the
proto-Niger-Congo society, we can reconstruct one particular
key indicator of the subsistence use of grains, an ancient root
word **pʰóndé for a grain species today called fonio, a very early
West African domestic grain and one of the crops collected wild
by people of the Ounjougou culture.[17] Currently, there is also one
relevant verb that we can track back to proto-Niger-Congo, **ba.
Most often the reflexes of this root that have been identified so far

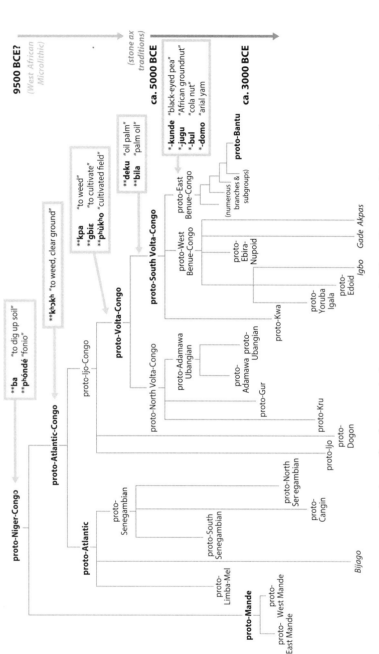

FIGURE 3.2. Lexicon of evolving agriculture among early Niger-Congo-speaking peoples.

do connote activities of cultivation. Its original meaning may, how-ever, have been more generally "to dig up"—for example, tubers—without necessarily implying cultivation.[18]

But from the second era of early Niger-Congo history—from the proto-Atlantic-Congo period onward—new additions to the lexicon become clearer in their implications. From that node onward a succession of new root words with meanings consis-tently indicative of a gradual shift toward the *deliberate* tending of crops appear at each major historical stage in the comparative lexical evidence. At the proto-Atlantic period a verb, $**k^h\mathfrak{d}k^h$, for clearing away competing vegetation from favored crops had come into use.[19] Two nodes later on the Niger-Congo family tree, at the proto-Volta-Congo period dating probably to around the seventh millennium BCE, cultivation practices appear to have finally come more fully into being. Marking this new stage in the transition to farming was the adoption of two new verbs in that period—one, $**$gbiɛ, for cultivation in general and the other, $**$kpa, specifically connoting weeding—along with a noun, $**p^hùk^ho$, meaning "cultivated field." Still more terms, notably for new kinds of crops, then came into use in the immediately following period of the early sixth millennium BCE, when, as argued previously, the stone ax–making proto-South Volta-Congo peoples expanded across the woodland savanna and rainforests zones from east-ern Ivory Coast to southern Cameroon.[20] Together these word histories suggest that the first steps toward deliberate tending and protection—that is to say, incipient *cultivation*—of wild grains may have begun not all that long after the invention of ceramic technology in the Ounjougou culture—over perhaps the next two thousand years, hence over the span from around 8500 down to 6000 BCE—with a fuller reliance on farming taking hold from 6000 onward.

These new words, diagnostic of cultivation-related prac-tices, came successively into use at periods *before* the available archaeology as yet can show the presence of fully domesticated versions, genetically speaking, of the West African crops. In part, this lack of evidence surely reflects the usual lag times of as much as one thousand to two thousand or more years between the time when people first begin to tend crops that are still genetically wild and the time that those crops eventually develop the genetic characteristics that confirm their full domestication. Equally significant in this case are the enormous gaps in our archaeological knowledge of the West Africa Sahel and Sudan geographical zones between 8500 and 5000 BCE. There must be hundreds and hundreds of sites of that period still to be discovered—sites that will eventually allow us to fill in our understanding of just how the long transition from foraging to cultivation—and eventually, over the still longer run, .to full plant domestication—proceeded over the *longue durée* in those parts of Africa.

The next nodal period, the proto-South Volta-Congo period, in the family tree of the history of Niger-Congo-speaking peoples marked a major new departure in these developments, with the early South Volta-Congo communities moving south from the more open West African savannas, inhabited by their immediate proto-Volta-Congo ancestors, into higher-rainfall woodland and rainforest environments. What allowed their advance into this different range of ecosystems? The reconstructed lexicon of crops offers some strong clues. The ancestral proto-South Volta-Congo people adapted to these different environments because they began to favor, as new additions to their agricultural lexicons indicate, oil palms and new kinds of yam—plants of the wetter wooded savannas and the rainforest (see fig. 3.2). In addition, the reconstructed lexicons indicate that they brought with them at least two crops domesticated in the savannas that proved adaptable to the wetter climates— cowpeas (black-eyed peas, *Vigna unguiculata*) and the African (or Bambara) groundnut (*Vigna subterranea*). Then, in the late fourth millennium and early third millennium BCE, a new

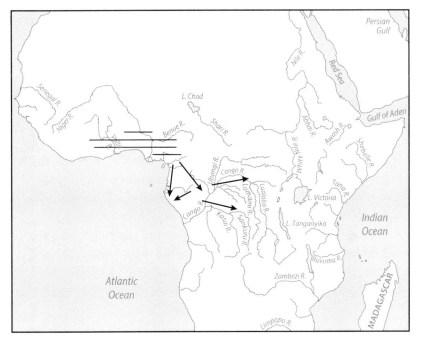

MAP 3.3. Stone axes and early expansions of Bantu speakers, 3000–1500 BCE (arrows). Horizontal lines refer to the area occupied by speakers of South Volta-Congo.

age in the expansion of South Volta-Congo societies began—of peoples speaking languages of the Bantu sub-branch of South Volta-Congo. The ancestral Bantu-speaking society was one among a number of South Volta-Congo societies that resided in the fourth millennium in what is today the country of Cameroon. The early Bantu communities advanced from southern Cameroon, spreading widely by settlement and linguistic adoption through the equatorial rainforest regions of Central Africa over the course of the third and second millennia, relying on stone axes and other tools (map 3.3).[21] Still later, in the centuries around the turn of the eras from BCE to CE, a final major era of expansion spread speakers of Bantu languages and their cultures across much of the rest of the southern third of Africa.[22]

In this long history from the beginning of the Holocene, gender roles would have figured prominently in still another manner, and not in the way that knowledge of European or Middle Eastern history might lead one to presume. All across the areas of early agriculture among Niger-Congo speakers, the comparative ethnographic evidence reveals women to have been the primary farmers. Men have commonly taken on the initial task of clearing land for cultivation; and in some areas, southern Nigeria for example, certain kinds of yams are considered a man's crop. But nearly everywhere it would have been women who prepared the soil and carried out the planting, weeding, and harvesting of most crops. All across those regions women would have been the prime movers of the shift, over those long millennia, from foraging to farming.

The Age of Agricultural Exchange

As the earliest farming societies in the world expanded farther and farther outward from their origin regions, sooner or later their expansions brought them into contact with other expanding, primary farming societies—with societies that were spreading their lands outward from their own independent centers of primary agricultural invention. And those encounters set in motion the second age of early agriculture, an age we can call the Age of Agricultural Exchange.[23]

The Age of Agricultural Exchange tended everywhere in world history to be very much an age of *multidirectional* exchange. In the case of Africa, early agricultural contributions passed from Africa to Eurasia as well as from Eurasia to Africa. But in the early stages far more contributions passed from Africa to Eurasia than the other way around. Africa was not some passive recipient region of the world but instead an active cultural donor to global history.

INTO AFRICA

As our starting point in assessing this history of early agricultural exchange, we turn to a second major, ancient African language family, Nilo-Saharan. The evolution of Nilo-Saharan lexicons relating to both the tending of animals and the raising of crops, and the historical inferences that follow from this evidence, have been explored in several previous works. The Nilo-Saharan family tree presented here (fig. 3.3) includes, as did the Niger-Congo tree (see fig. 3.2), notations about new words relating to food production that came into use at each successive nodal period in the history of the language family.[24]

The combined lexical and archaeological evidence suggests that the Nilo-Saharan speakers of the eastern Sahara may have begun already, at the proto-Northern Sudanic period of the late ninth or early eighth millennium BCE, to take some first steps toward cattle domestication, perhaps protecting and looking after the welfare of the indigenous wild cattle in one or another fashion (see Northern Sudanic node in figure 3.3 for the relevant verbs dating to that era).[25] In the following period, the proto-Saharo-Sahelian era, proposed to date to the second half of the eighth millennium BCE, the local communities of this region shifted to a sedentary way of life. The proto-Saharo-Sahelian lexical evidence for economic and social change accords in detail with a particular range of archaeological changes dating to this period in the eastern Sahara. The lexical evidence reveals that these communities began to reside in neighborhoods of homesteads, each surrounded by a thornbush pen for the protection of cattle from predators at night. A notable innovation of the time, attested in the linguistic evidence and confirmed in the archaeology, was the first building of round houses with conical roofs, a style widely prevalent among Nilo-Saharan speakers down to recent centuries.[26]

The archaeology and the linguistic evidence also combine in indicating the beginning, at the same period, of the shift from

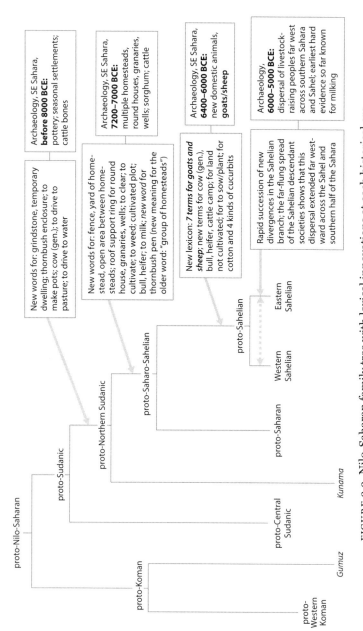

FIGURE 3.3. Nilo-Saharan family tree with lexical innovations at each historical era, with the parallel archaeological sequence.

foraging to cultivation of crops. The words newly in use in that era include three verbs for cultivating activities, along with nouns for a cultivated field and for a pit granary, with the latter item also newly attested in the archaeology of just that period.[27] The excavated granaries of the late eighth millennium contained sorghum grains indistinguishable from those of wild sorghum, in keeping with the inference that the proto-Saharo-Sahelian speakers were still at the initiatory stages of the shift to food production.

In the body of evidence in figure 3.3, the next particular node on the family tree, the proto-Sahelian node, stands out for two reasons, one having to do with the topic of agricultural exchange and the other having to do with historical chronology. First, the proto-Sahelian language added *seven* new words relating to goats and sheep, both animals domesticated in the Levant, and to their life stages. Life-stage terminology is proof positive of a society's herding and breeding of the animals in question. In addition, a strain of domesticated cattle of eastern Mediterranean origin apparently spread to the proto-Sahelian communities in the same era as the goats and sheep. In keeping with the lexical evidence for the protecting of indigenous cattle as early as the eighth millennium, the genetic evidence also indicates interbreeding between the local and the introduced cattle.[28]

Second, and most important for the chronology of agricultural exchange, in the archaeology of the southern eastern Sahara—in just the areas where the proto-Sahelian language would have been spoken—ovicaprids (sheep and goats) first turn up between around 6400 and 6000 BCE.[29] The new words at the proto-Sahelian era for, in particular, sheep and goats and their life-stages (see again fig. 3.3) thus allow us to date the proto-Sahelian society to sometime around or immediately before 6000 BCE. The combined archaeological and lexical evidence shows that, for the peoples of the southern eastern Sahara and for northeastern Africa more broadly, the Age of Agricultural Exchange with another region of agricultural innovation, the Levant, began by or shortly before 6000 BCE.

The addition, also at the proto-Sahelian era, of new words for cattle life stages indicate that, parallel with the adoption of goats and sheep, an overall shift to a more intensive reliance on pastoral pursuits was surely under way—a finding again in keeping with the Saharan archaeological evidence of the period from 6000 BCE onward. Interestingly, the innovation in proto-Sahelian of a word denoting an outlying cattle camp suggests the emergence, by this time already, of a particular customary practice reflective of intensive pastoralism, still followed among some recent Nilo-Saharan speaking societies, such as the Turkana of northern Kenya. According to this practice, the young men each year drive the herds out to distant pastures during the wet season and then bring them back in the dry season to reserved pastures near the sedentary family homesteads of the community.

OUT OF AFRICA

But what if we look in the opposite direction, outward from Africa toward Eurasia?

What we discover is that a much larger variety of items, in particular crops domesticated deep in Africa, very early spread from Africa to the Middle East and, from the Middle East, often to still more distant regions. The northward spread out of Africa of at least *twelve* crops from south of the Sahara—along with one domestic animal—was under way almost as early as the spread of goats and sheep southward.

At least four African crops—watermelons, bottle gourds, muskmelons, and cowpeas[30]—spread north to Egypt as early as the fourth and third millennia BCE, and subsequently from Egypt into the Middle East and far beyond. Africans of the Sudan belt of Africa were the source of the watermelon and the bottle gourd. The origins of the muskmelon—the progenitor in later times of numerous cultivated varieties, including cantaloupes, honeydew, casaba, Crenshaw, and Persian melons, among others—have sometimes in the past been a matter of debate. But the distributions of the wild ancestor of all the varieties of this crop confirm its eastern African origins: wild muskmelons occur from Eritrea southward to Tanzania. And the Horn of Africa, as the earliest part of these regions to develop agriculture, stands out as surely the origin region of cultivated muskmelons.

By the third millennium BCE a widening spread of crops out of Africa was under way. A region of especially important early African impact was the Indian subcontinent. The people of the Harappan culture of the Indus region had already cultivated a suite of five African crops before 2000 BCE:[31]

> *pearl (*or *bulrush) millet*, apparently domesticated separately in both the western and eastern parts of the Sudan belt of Africa;
> *sorghum* and the *lablab bean*, both of these crops domesticated in the eastern Sudan;
> *finger millet*, domesticated in the Ethiopian Highlands by Cushitic speakers; and
> *cowpeas*, domesticated in West Africa by Niger-Congo-speaking peoples.[32]

Sorghum spread still farther, far beyond India, all the way to northern China, where it became one of the primary crops of northern Chinese agriculture. It arrived there possibly as early as 3000 BCE,[33] but certainly no later than 1000 BCE. The lablab bean spread far and wide as well, right across southern Asia to Vietnam and to China.

An associated, especially interesting historical problem is the question of how these five crops, and especially the notable African grains, sorghum, pearl millet, and finger millet, reached India by or before the second millennium BCE, apparently without passing first through the Middle East. Early seagoing trade is the likely intermediary in this transmission. In the third millennium the communities of Oman had already an established seagoing tradition, as had the people of the Harappan tradition of the Indus and Gujarat regions. The latter regions were particularly well suited by climate for the incoming African crops. The most probable history, as the evidence stands, is that these crops were taken across the Red Sea from the Horn of Africa to southern Arabia by or before 3000 BCE. After becoming established in Yemen and Oman, these crops were then transported by sea from Oman to the Indian subcontinent even before the end of the third millennium BCE. As the work of the archaeologist Dorian Fuller and his colleagues reveals, the spread of these crops brings to light a key emerging sphere of long-distance, intercontinental connections dating back more than four thousand years and linking Africa via southern Arabia to South Asia. These are connections about which historians have almost everything still to learn.[34]

Two additional West African contributions to world agriculture diffused widely out of the continent, probably also along those sea routes and possibly just as early. One was a tuber crop, the country potato (*Plectranthus rotundifolia*). It spread to India and across southern Asia, eventually as far as China.[35] A second crop, the roselle (*Hibiscus sabdariffa*), spread even more widely. Its rather spicy leaves have typically been used in sauces and soups, not just in West African cuisines, but in India and across Southeast Asia. Hibiscus tea is made from the sepals of the roselle fruit.

The West African contributions to the Age of Agricultural Exchange included, as well, a fruit tree species—the tamarind. This tree took on particularly notable importance in India, but also spread from there to Island South Asia. And, of course, the castor-oil plant, which originated in the Horn of Africa and had already spread by the third millennium, if not earlier, to Egypt, came eventually to have an almost worldwide distribution.

Not only plants, but also one particularly notable animal—the donkey—came to the rest of the world from Africa. Modern cultural attitudes toward the donkey make it easy for present-day folk to underestimate the historical significance of donkey domestication. We have been faced, after all, with centuries of Westerners treating the "lowly ass" as an object of ridicule and using its name to slander individuals as stupid. But in the context of deep history, this attitude completely misses the immense significance of this animal. The donkey was the first multiple-use beast of burden in world history—for carrying loads, for riding, and, in the Middle East, very early put to use pulling wheeled vehicles. The possession of donkeys was essential to the earliest carrying of goods over long distances for trade as well as to the emergence of the first wheeled transport in history, and the uses that people made of the donkey very likely served as the models for the subsequent domestication and utilization of horses and camels.

So who domesticated the donkey? The genetic evidence for donkeys indicates that communities in Somaliland in the Horn of Africa and also farther north along the Red Sea Hills apparently separately participated in the domestication of this important animal.[36] In both regions the local people would have spoken early languages of the Cushitic branch of the Afrasian family, and in that branch we can track a word distinguishing domestic donkeys from wild donkeys back to a period roughly in the range of 5000 BCE,[37] consistent with the genetic dating of domestic donkeys and with their appearance after 4000 BCE in the archaeological record in Egypt.[38]

From the Cushitic-speaking peoples of the Red Sea Hills regions the domestic donkey spread northward via Egypt to southwestern Asia. With the arrival of donkeys, the cities of ancient Mesopotamia and the Levant acquired a new and valued means for carrying goods over long distances and for pulling wheeled vehicles no later than the early fourth millennium BCE. Consider the item depicted in figure 3.4.[39] This is a Sumerian cylinder seal of the fourth millennium BCE relating to the early importance of the donkey and dating well before the first introduction of domestic horses south of the Caucasus and the Black Sea. The central portion of this seal depicts a chariot with its

FIGURE 3.4. Sumerian cylinder seal, fourth millennium BCE, depicting chariots pulled by donkeys.

rider, being pulled by an ass, whose reins the rider holds. This chariot follows a second chariot, of which we see only the back wheels and the rider; while behind the main chariot we see the figure of an ass pulling still a third, unseen chariot. These are not chariots as we think of them from later eras. They have solid wheels, with no spokes. The museum notes do describe the central vehicle as a "war chariot," but its cumbersome wheels rather suggest that we are instead dealing here with a prestige vehicle rather than, as yet, with practical war weaponry.

Donkeys, as the earliest animals to carry trade goods over distances and to pull vehicles, were the likely models and impetus for the subsequent domestication of an indigenous southwestern Asian animal, the camel, and for its use both for riding and in short- and long-distance transport. It seems also possible that the arrival of at least knowledge of the donkey in the Pontic steppes sometime in the fourth millennium BCE may have served as an impetus for change among the early Indo-Europeans, who began in that millennium to use the horse as no longer just a meat source but also to carry people and goods and to pull wagons.[40]

So, overall, in the Age of Agricultural Exchange of the seventh to the fourth millennium BCE, Africa was not a passive, recipient continent. On the contrary, Africans were active contributors to new developments in the wider world, sending far more new things outward than they received back. At least eleven different food crops—along with a nonfood crop, the castor-oil plant—in addition to the donkey spread in the opposite direction, from Africa often far into Eurasia before, and possibly sometimes well before, 2000 or 3000 BCE.

It is worth reemphasizing again that these thirteen contributions came from several different centers of innovation well south in Africa:

> *watermelons* and also the *bottle gourd* broadly from the Sudan belt of Africa;
> *muskmelons* from the Horn of Africa;
> *cowpeas*, the *country potato*, *roselle*, and also the *tamarind*, from West Africa;
> *pearl millet* from both the western and eastern parts of the Sudan belt;
> *sorghum* and the *lablab bean*, from the eastern Sahara and eastern Sudan;
> *finger millet* from Cushitic-speaking peoples living in the Ethiopian highlands;
> the *castor-oil plant* most probably from the Horn of Africa, also from Cushitic speakers; and
> the *donkey* from Cushitic-speaking inhabitants of the dry steppe and semidesert lands of the far eastern Sahara and northern fringe of the Ethiopian Highlands.

What the varied origin lands of these African contributions tell us is that, already by or before 5000 to 3000 BCE, interregional connections began, more and more, to shape the wider trends of cultural and economic exchange within the continent. The spread in this era of crops of West African origin eastward across the Sudan belt of Africa—and in the most easterly areas becoming part of the spread of agricultural innovations outward from Africa into Eurasia—is a particularly notable marker of this emerging historical age.

An equally notable marker of these growing interregional connections within Africa was the countervailing, westward spread across the continent of several kinds of domestic animals during that same time span. As reconstructed word histories from Niger-Congo as well as Nilo-Saharan and Afrasian languages reveal, goats and cattle had spread from the eastern Sudan regions far across West Africa as early as the fifth and fourth millennia BCE.[41] And as the developments recounted in chapter 4 reveal, the donkey, domesticated far to the east by Africans of the Red Sea Hills and northern fringe of the Ethiopian Highlands, may have been introduced to the western and central Sudan regions equally early.[42]

Significant agricultural innovations did, in more limited ways, spread in the opposite direction, from Eurasia to Africa. Two notable animals, goats and sheep, as we have seen, had diffused along with additional cattle from the Levant to northeastern Africa as early as the seventh millennium, and sheep and goats in particular eventually became important and spread widely across most of the continent.

But other Eurasian contributions had a less wide impact on Africa. By the seventh and sixth millennia BCE, Levantine crops, notably barley and early wheat varieties, were diffusing along the northern fringe of the continent, with its similar Mediterranean climate and winter rains, and to some parts of Egypt, such as the Fayum, where irrigation allowed their cultivation. In addition, sometime before the full drying of the Sahara, probably in the fourth millennium, a further spread of these crops, including wheat, barley, and chickpeas, passed southeastward into the highlands of the Horn of Africa, to modern-day Eritrea and northern Ethiopia.[43] In these more southerly regions of northeastern Africa, the crops benefited from the cool-season rains of the highlands, which provided conditions much like the winter-rain regimes of the southwestern Asian lands from which those crops had originally come.

The lexical evidence shows that these Levantine crops reached the Horn of Africa, not from across the Red Sea, but apparently from Egypt, via the Red Sea Hills, which in some locales were still marginally arable until around 3300 BCE. The Cushitic-speaking peoples of the highlands adopted these crops into their existing agriculture practices, which had centered previously around the cultivation of two indigenous highland grain crops, finger millet and teff.[44]

An additional southwestern Asian agricultural innovation of restricted spread was the plow. It reached the highlands of the Horn along with the Middle Eastern crops, and in time became the primary implement of cultivation in the northern and central, and some parts of the southern, Ethiopian Highlands.[45] But in the Sudan belt and farther south in East Africa, tropical warm-season rain regimes and different soil conditions limited the further spread of these various agricultural introductions.

These histories bring us once again to points already raised in chapters 1 and 2. They remind us that developments in ancient historical periods of world history moved ahead in Africa along similar historical vectors and did so during the same broad ages as among the peoples of other continents—in technology, in agricultural history, and, as is considered in chapters 4 and 5, in the emergence of commerce, towns, and states. One cannot fully understand, for instance, the emergence of towns and complex society in India if we do not take into account the fundamental African contributions to the evolution of agricultural ways of life in the subcontinent. And Africans were the domesticators of the donkey, an animal that became a major stimulus for change outside the continent, with a fundamental impact on early trade history across large parts of ancient Eurasia, as well as westward across Sudan belt of Africa. Donkey domestication had a seminal impact, I would argue, on the global history of animal transport and wheeled transport, serving as a model for camel domestication and, possibly, for the use of horses for riding and for wheeled-vehicle transport.

CHAPTER FOUR

Towns and Long-Distance Commerce in Ancient Africa

The West African Commercial Revolution

In the West African savanna belt south of the Sahara the rise of the first towns and the development of commerce over distance were conjoined developments. They were part and parcel of what we might call the West African Commercial Revolution. These developments took shape over roughly the same broad span of time as another notable early commercial revolution of world historical significance—one that had its origins in the eastern Mediterranean and Levant.[1] Both these *initially quite separate* commercial revolutions had their beginnings in the second millennium BCE.

What do I mean by "commercial revolution"? The transforming feature of the Mediterranean and Levantine commercial revolution was the shift from kings' agents or temple agents as the primary managers of distance trade to an emerging new economic class—merchants—who became more and more widely the primary suppliers and carriers of goods. Along with this shift in the relations of trade, there came the emergence of a new kind of town. Previously towns, where they did exist, as in Egypt and in the Levant and Mesopotamia, were principally temple centers and/or the governing centers of kingdoms. The new kind of town served instead primarily as a production center of goods destined for commerce or else as a trading center located at the crossroads of trade routes from one region to another, or as both.

What is generally not recognized outside of the African sphere—and only too often not even by historians of Africa—is the importance of the separate commercial revolution that was under way in the western and central Sudan belt of Africa during the second and first millennia BCE. It began independently of the developments of the Mediterranean region. This separate African commercial revolution—this shift to organized long-distance trade carried on by professional traders—appears in fact to have begun even earlier in time. Four centers of production of goods for trade emerged in the western and central Sudan belt of Africa by no later than the early and middle second millennium BCE (map 4.1). It was the linking up of the production of these regions in the second half of the second millennium BCE that progressively brought the West African commercial revolution into existence.

The best-studied center of the new kinds of production is the Tichit region, located in today's southern Mauritania, close to the Mali border and 500 kilometers west-northwest of the inland delta of the Niger River. In the Tichit region between 1800 and 1200 BCE there developed a string of towns, with one larger than the rest toward the middle of this skein. Families of skilled artisans in each of the towns engaged in the manufacture of different particular products for trade—with the different towns tending to specialize in different items—arrowheads in one, grindstones in another, carnelian beads in yet another, and so forth. And these towns appear to have traded not just with each other, but with regions hundreds of kilometers away,

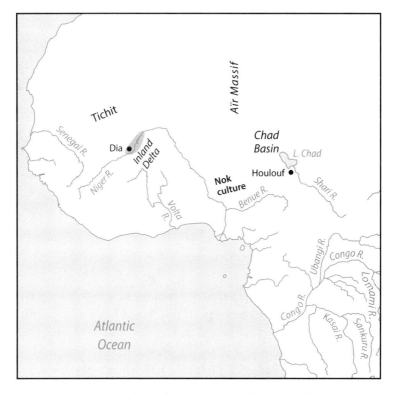

MAP 4.1. Early production areas of the West African commercial revolution.

both to the east and the west.[2] Figure 4.1 shows part of the stone ruins of one of those towns, of the period 1800 to 1200 BCE.[3]

A second seminal region in the West African commercial revolution in the second millennium BCE comprised the areas both in and surrounding the inland delta of the Niger. The delta region encompassed a range of highly contrasting environments for subsistence production. Right along its bayous lived communities of fishing specialists. In the dry land areas among the channels of the Niger there resided a different set of communities—specialists in the cultivation of African rice. And, finally, for hundreds of kilometers all around the delta there

FIGURE 4.1. Ruins of a town in Tichit, 1800–1200 BCE.

lived communities engaged in dry farming of a variety of African grains other than rice—pearl millet and fonio, along with sorghum, which by that period had spread westward from the eastern Sudan belt—and in raising livestock. As the archaeologists Susan and Roderick McIntosh have shown, the multidirectional exchange of subsistence products among the different specialist communities of the inland delta, as well as between them and the farming populations of the surrounding Sahel and savanna, goes far back into the past, well before the second millennium BCE.[4]

A third major contributing region to the West African commercial revolution lay in the Aïr Mountains, located at the southernmost edge of the Sahara, 1,200 kilometers to the east of the inland delta, in the modern-day country of Niger. As we learned in chapter 2, between around 2500 and 1500 BCE, the inhabitants of Aïr experimented with the smelting of local copper—bringing into being a fully operational industry of copper smelting no later than 1500 BCE. With that development, the Aïr region soon became the exporter of copper far and wide across the central as well as the western Sudan belt.

In Aïr itself significant urban development may not have taken place until later. But something else quite notable did happen. In five different parts of Aïr, people in this era began to construct megalithic grave sites. The archaeologist Augustin Holl has proposed that these sites indicate the existence of possibly five different small polities by the centuries 1500 to 1000 BCE—each ruling over a portion of the copper-bearing lands of the massif.[5]

Even before the end of the second millennium and beginning of the first millennium BCE, all these regions began to be linked together in expanding networks of commercial exchange. Across the Sahel of today's Mali a new kind of town grew out of what had originally been clusters of manufacturing villages. One village or ward of the newly evolving town was inhabited by weavers of cotton textiles for the market. We don't know yet how early cotton weaving had spread westward into West Africa, but clearly before the end of the second millennium the technology was fully established there. Leather-working families inhabited another ward of the town, and still another ward was the habitation of professional potting families. And, finally, in the first millennium BCE, as knowledge of iron technology reached as far west as Mali, each town came to include a fourth ward, inhabited by ironworking specialist families.[6] The fifth element in the new urban populations consisted of the emerging merchant class, who carried, and financed the carrying of, the products of the town to distant places. Over the course of the late second and the first millennia BCE, the expansion of long-distance trade took place not just across today's Mali and Senegal, but as far east as the Chad basin of modern Niger, northern Nigeria, and Chad. One notable early town, Dia, its origins dating to the close of the second millennium BCE, lay at the west side of the inland delta of the Niger River.[7] Far to the east, Houlouf on Lake Chad (see map 4.1) grew into a notable polity and intersection point in the growing networks of trade.[8] Archaeologists have identified several hundred probable and possible town sites, spread across the nearly 2,000 kilometers of the western and central Sudan belt—sites that are going to occupy the attention of generations of future archaeologists.[9]

The independent commercial revolution of the western and central Sudan regions rests ultimately on two major sets of historical developments that we have already considered. One of these was the transition to fully agricultural ways of life. Agriculture, because of its ability to produce vastly more food than foraging from the same amount of land, everywhere enabled the growth of human population overall. More important, a new kind of specialization, in the trading of the products of farming, became essential to feeding the concentrated populations of the towns.

The second set of foundational events was technological. The inventions of ceramics, loom weaving of cotton, and metallurgy well before this time, as described in chapter 2, gave the inhabitants of the towns the capacities for manufacturing the wares of commerce, the goods on which were built the prosperity and growth of towns all across the western and central Sudan belt in the later second and the first millennia BCE.

In these regions as well, the donkey played a significant role. Brought west by peoples speaking languages of the Chadic branch of the Afrasian language family,[10] this animal seems likely to have been an established beast of burden across a wide stretch of the southern Sahara from probably before the end of the fifth millennium BCE. In the second and first millennia BCE donkeys became key carriers in the overland transport of goods in the emerging commercial networks, with boat transport along the Niger River providing another major avenue of the movement of goods over long distances.

One not-at-all-tangential misconception about the primary history of long-distance commerce in West Africa needs direct confrontation here. There is a tendency for scholars to attribute to the Garamantes, notable African merchants of the northern and middle parts of the central Sahara in the mid-first millennium BCE, an instigating role in the West African commercial revolution. This view betrays the presumption once again of Africans south of the Sahara as peripheral—as people not acting but acted upon. But the chronology of these histories refutes this idea straight out. The Garamantes began to become prominent only from the ninth and eighth centuries BCE onward. The two commercial revolutions—to the north in the Mediterranean regions, and to the south in the western and central Sudan belt—were each already separately under way centuries earlier, in the second millennium BCE.

It is the Garamantes who began as peripheral actors. They lived on the southern periphery of the Mediterranean and Middle Eastern commercial revolution. They lived on the northern periphery of the West African commercial revolution. They were responders, not instigators. They responded to commercial opportunities—to the availability of goods that reached them from both the savanna lands of Africa to the south and the Mediterranean Sea lanes to the north—although they began soon also to produce products of their own for both market regions.[11]

A Second African Commercial Revolution: The Congo Basin

West Africa was not the only region of early emerging commercial networks in the continent. Even farther south, the Congo basin in the heart of equatorial Africa was home as well, and not all that many centuries later, to a second major African network of interconnected exchange relations over long distances. In the Congo basin the primary routes of commerce followed the numerous large rivers, with the traders from Bantu-speaking farming and fishing communities moving their goods upriver and downriver by boat (map 4.2). Secondary feeder routes followed paths through the surrounding rainforests to the rivers, with the Batwa foraging peoples (the so-called Pygmies) especially

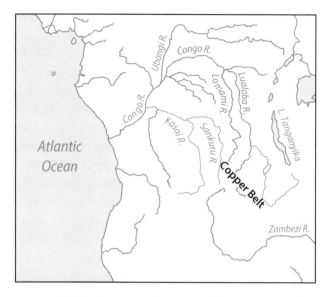

MAP 4.2. Major river connections of early commerce in the Congo basin.

carrying forest products, such as hides, ivory, beeswax, and honey, along those tracks.

Our knowledge of these developments rests in particular on the studies carried out by Jan Vansina and Kairn Klieman. What we know best are the developments of the past two thousand years, but Klieman has shown that the beginnings of the long-distance transport of goods in these regions very likely go back to early in the first millennium BCE.[12] Ironworking, as we have seen, spread from the Western Rift regions westward and south-westward along these routes during the middle and the second half of that millennium.

At least one domestic animal, the sheep, dispersed out from the African Great Lakes region, following these same routes, apparently beginning also in the first millennium BCE. One line of the spread of sheep raising, marked by the diffusion from language to language of a particular word, *-meme, for "sheep," passed west from peoples living in the far southeastern parts of today's South Sudan, who spoke languages of the Central Sudanic branch of the Nilo-Saharan family (see fig. 3.3). The diffusion of this word tracks the spread of sheep from those peoples southwestward through the Bantu-speaking areas along the middle Congo River and from there to the Atlantic coast around the mouth of the Congo River. A second line of the spread of sheep, revealed in the distribution of a Great Lakes Bantu word for the animal, *-panga, passed during the same time span from the early Bantu settlers of the African Great Lakes southwestward to the Bantu societies of the regions around and south of the upper and middle Sankuru River (see map 4.2).[13]

Then, in the early first millennium CE, African smiths spread the knowledge of a notable new set of developments in iron-forging technology, with the new techniques again tending especially to disperse along the river routes of the Congo basin. Jan Vansina has called these developments the "second" iron age of Africa.

One notable product that came out of these technological advances was the flange-welded double bell. To make a double bell, the smith had first to forge four flat iron sheets; then reheat the iron sheets to a high temperature in the forge and hammer each, placed upon a rounded form, into a curved half-bell shape, with a flat flange extending out all around the curved central portion of the sheet; next, weld together in the fire of the forge the flanges of the two halves of each bell; and, finally, forge and weld onto the top of the two bells a curved iron handle, attaching them to each other. Figure 4.2 is a modern example made by a smith living in the northwestern parts of the equatorial rainforest region, proving that this technological tradition was still very much alive as late as the nineteenth century CE.

Above and beyond its technological implications, the flange-welded double bell is historically significant for an additional, very different reason: the spread of this implement reveals a political consequence of the rise of the Congo basin commercial links,

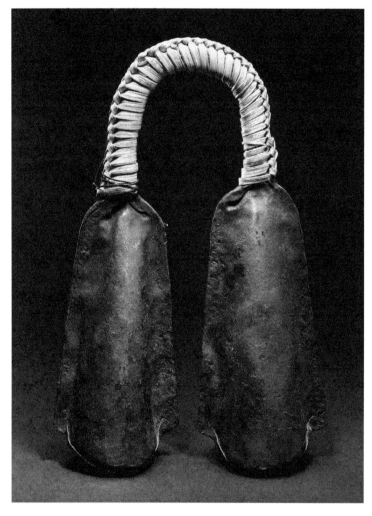

FIGURE 4.2. Flange-welded double bell, nineteenth century CE.

namely, the emergence of chiefdoms and very small states along the main lines, and especially at juncture points, of the commercial connections of the first millennium BCE and first millennium CE.[14] The smiths produced this item to serve as part of the regalia of the ruler of such a polity. Each bell of the pair had a different pitch, with one bell emitting a higher-pitched sound than the other. Because the Bantu languages are generally two-tone languages, any phrase or saying will present a particular sequence of high and low tones in its words. For this reason the carrier of the bells for a king or chief could strike them so as to play the tonal sequence of the words in a standard saying or phrase that invoked political or ritual authority. The hearers, knowing the phrase well, would know from the pitch sequence of the striking of the bells just which phrase was being conveyed. As Jan Vansina has shown, the combined linguistic and archaeological evidence reveals that the double bells already had spread widely across the Congo basin during the first millennium CE and, by the very early second millennium across the Zambezi basin as far south as the lands that were, in the thirteenth to fifteenth centuries, to become the empire of Great Zimbabwe.[15]

An additional new set of items representative also of this particular technological advance was throwing knives, composed often of several forged blades welded together into one complex weapon. The earliest throwing knives may have been made in the Darfur region of the modern-day country of Sudan, but over the course of the first and second millennia CE this kind of implement came to have a much wider distribution than even the double bells. They spread to peoples along the Ubangi watershed north of Congo basin proper (see map 4.2) as well as all across the Congo basin itself.[16] Figure 4.3 shows a particularly striking product of this technological expertise, a throwing knife from the Zande people of the upper Uele River watershed of the Ubangi River. Already in the early first millennium CE, the Bantu-speaking lands in and around the Upemba depression, through which the Lualaba River flowed, had become major producing areas of iron and iron goods and of salt, with both kinds of products being traded northward, initially along the Lualaba and Lomami Rivers, into the networks of the central Congo basin.

FIGURE 4.3. Zande throwing knife.

Developments in the first four centuries CE added a new factor to these resources. Ironworking Bantu people living south of the Upemba depression, at the southern edges of the Congo basin, took advantage of the rich deposits of copper ores in the region of southern Congo and northern Zambia that came to be called, in the twentieth century, the "Copper Belt" (see map 4.2)—they independently invented copper smelting in that region. From the miners and smelters of this region copper passed northward along the rivers of the Congo basin, as well as southward through the Zambezi River basin.

An associated social feature of the wider Congo basin commercial revolution was the institution of so-called secret societies— associations composed of the merchants who carried out the trade and also other leading figures from the chiefdoms and small kingdoms involved in the wider networks of commercial relations. Women as well as men could belong. These societies existed across most of the eastern half of the Congo basin—extending in the west from the areas along the length of the Lomami River eastward to Lake Tanganyika. The societies were "secret" in much in the same way that Masonic societies are secret. And they were similar to the Masons in having ranks ("degrees" in the case of Masons) through which the members could advance upward. Particular rituals marked one's advancement in rank, and there were different rituals to participate in once one had attained particular status.

The presence of these institutions enabled a merchant traveling with goods to call upon the hospitality and protection of local communities in each of the areas the merchant traveled to. This accommodation was possible because in each area the merchant could find members either of the same society or of a society allied to the merchant's own society. These relations served to protect and facilitate the passage of goods over great distances and through a skein of independent chiefdoms and small kingdoms, even when those polities might otherwise be at odds with each other.[17]

How far back in time do these institutional relationships go? The "secret" societies that facilitated trade in the upper and middle Congo River regions certainly already existed in the early second millennium or later first millennium CE. But for the still earlier periods of long-distance trade in the Congo basin—in the first millennium BCE and very early first millennium CE—the institutions and relations that facilitated and protected trade remain to be discovered.

Commercial "Revolutions" in the Global Frame

In the wider framework of world history, these early systems and networks of long-distance exchange in Africa and elsewhere, because they emerged out of different cultural and social worlds, had historical consequences both similar and different. A common consequence globally of what I describe here as commercial revolutions has been the eventual emergence of currencies. Currency served as tokens of value to recompense sellers or buyers when the products that the sellers or buyers wished to obtain in exchange were not available or not in sufficient supply. In each region currencies came into use, not at the first stages of the commercial revolutions, but usually centuries later, as exchange relations matured and became more complex and more varied in the range products traded.

Historians have long given attention to the emergence of currency in the form of coinage from the seventh century BCE onward in the eastern Mediterranean regions. But for a truly global perspective historians need to take into account not just coinage, but all the varieties of currencies that peoples in different regions of the world developed and how those currencies functioned. The African commercial networks of West Africa put into use a currency in the form of small copper ingots, of standardized size. We know of these from the beginning of the first millennium CE, but their use may well go back centuries earlier. Standard weights of gold dust served also relatively early as a currency in West Africa.[18] In the interior Congo basin copper currency in the shape of a cross came into use, possibly as early as the fourth century CE. And this currency continued to be used right down to the beginning of the colonial era in the late nineteenth century. In the Lower Congo River region, a different early currency long existed: nzimbu shells. We do not yet know for how far back in time these shells served as currency, but they are the kind of items that are preserved well in the archaeology, so there is surely much more to be learned about the history of their use.

What is also apparent from the histories considered here is that different social and political trajectories have lain behind the rise of commercial networks in different regions. In the Middle East and Egypt, for example, small-scale worlds gave rise to a world of states and socially unequal societies long *before* the growing shift in the first millennium BCE toward merchant-based kinds of trade. The peoples of the western and central Sudan belt of Africa, on the other hand, followed a different historical pathway, beginning their shift as early as the second millennium BCE to a cultural world that included towns and new social classes of merchants and artisans. There the driving new factor was the emergence of specialized manufacturing and the exchange of manufactured goods for both the manufactures and raw materials of other, more distant areas. Only subsequently, in the early first millennium CE, did powerful empires, such as Wagadu, begin to arise in West Africa, building their power and wealth on controlling and protecting the already existing commercial relations.

These differences in how the Mediterranean and West African commercial revolutions came into being bring attention to another aspect important for world historical studies—that the overall historical trajectories toward our shared modern-day world followed different and often contrasting pathways in different regions of the world. Human beings, even when faced with comparable challenges, have responded sometimes in parallel fashions, sometimes in alternative manners. We have encountered this issue previously in the consideration of early technological advances in Africa (chapter 2), the variety of kinds of food production Africans brought into being, and how those developments may have played out differently from similar developments elsewhere (chapter 3). And we see it here in how complex networks of commercial relations came into being in different world regions.

How much have different human responses to comparable challenges been shaped by differences in natural environments? How much was it because people in different places in the world possessed different organizing ideas and explanations about the nature and meaning of existence? How much was it because of differences in the systems of social relations and the cultural expectations within which people had previously carried on their lives? Looking into these kinds of matters greatly enriches what we can learn and what we can teach about humankind and about the worlds we all came out of. And, once again, the developments of this age in the African continent show the crucial importance of taking Africa into account if we wish to make our world history truly global.

CHAPTER FIVE

The Africanity of Ancient Egypt

ANCIENT EGYPT WAS *in* Africa. More important, ancient Egypt was *of* Africa.

That is not the way that the previous two centuries of Western scholarship have presented this history. For too long ancient Egypt has been portrayed as if it were an offshoot of earlier Middle Eastern developments, as a region of somehow intrusive peoples coming from somewhere outside of Africa. It is long past the time for us all to discard these old notions—rooted as they are in the self-serving racialist presumptions of nineteenth-century Europeans—notions that too many people still today simply assume and never think to examine. The most recent generation of scholars and scholarship on Nubia and Egypt have been uncovering extensive new bodies of evidence, and they are casting aside the older assumptions and following where the evidence leads.

The older ideas do linger on, though, and scholars from other fields of study, not versed in the newer findings, and older Egyptologists as well, may still presume those views. There is, for example, a recent genetics article proposing that ancient Egyptians were of Levantine background.[1] But those findings come from a solitary northern, late ancient Egyptian locale—a site dating to more than two thousand years after the foundational period of ancient Egypt—and located in an area of Egypt that had by that time a history of more than a thousand years of the recurrent immigration of individuals and communities from the Levant into Egypt. These immigrants included, among others, communities of artisans and producers of valued goods—settlements encouraged by the rulers of Egypt. The military invasion of the Hyksos, coming from the Levant in the seventeenth century BCE, and their rule for more than a century over large parts of northern Egypt would also have brought an additional genetic component of Levantine background into those northern Egyptian regions.[2] The level of disconnect between the proposals made in this particular genetics article and the actual history of ancient Egyptian populations is the same as if one examined DNA from human remains in a late-nineteenth-century cemetery in South Boston, Massachusetts, and then concluded from that localized, time-bound sample, that Americans are basically of Irish descent and that the founders of the United States in the eighteenth century would have been primarily Irish, too.[3]

In any case, the geographical setting of the foundational developments of ancient Egyptian history in fact lay in lands well south of the single, late northern site considered in the genetics article. These lands extended from several hundred kilometers south of the confluence of the White Nile and the Abbai (or "Blue Nile") Rivers northward to the archaeological sites around El-Badari in Middle Egypt, 1,500 kilometers farther north. It was this vast stretch of lands—and not the northern areas of later Egyptian history—that constituted the foundational cultural regions and the cultural heartland of ancient Egypt.

The physical anthropological findings from the major burial sites of those founding locales of ancient Egypt in the fourth millennium BCE, notably El-Badari as well as Naqada, show *no* demographic indebtedness to the Levant. They reveal instead a population with cranial and dental features with closest parallels to those of other longtime populations of the surrounding areas of northeastern Africa, such as Nubia and the northern Horn of Africa. Members of this population did not come from somewhere else but were descendants of the long-term inhabitants of these portions of Africa going back many millennia.[4]

The Deep Background of Ancient Egyptian History, 20,000–6000 BCE

The history presented here is the history of Egypt's foundations as it is now told by the cohort of archaeologists who, over the past thirty years, have so greatly expanded and reshaped our historical knowledge of those regions and times. The evidence of physical anthropology and from linguistics only further adds to and backs up those findings.

There are, it turns out, two ancient Egyptian foundational stories to tell. One of these we might call the deep-time story—the history of developments and influences from 6000 to 3100 BCE. And then there is also what one might call the *very*-deep-time story, with its beginnings dating to before 15,000 BCE. The first task, historically speaking, is to set the deeper background: the very-deep-time story. Delving into that history requires a mix of historical approaches—comparative linguistic and comparative cultural evidence in coordination with archaeology.

To begin the linguistic and cultural historical excavation of this topic I must set out, first of all, the language relationships of ancient Egyptian. Ancient Egyptian, as noted, belonged to the Afrasian language family.[5] The primary question to pursue is chronological: When did the particular early Afrasian language directly ancestral to ancient Egyptian come to be spoken in the areas around and along the Egyptian Nile? But answering that question requires first answering two other questions:

Where does ancient Egyptian fit in the family tree of the Afrasian language family?

And where were the languages of the family spoken at different earlier points along the lines of linguistic descent in that family tree?

Regarding the first of these questions, the most recent findings show that the proto-Afrasian language diverged initially into two daughter languages, proto-Omotic and proto-Erythraic.[6] Proto-Erythraic in turn further diverged into two daughters of its own, proto-Cushitic and proto-North Erythraic. Still later in time, the proto-North Erythraic language itself diverged into two daughter languages, namely, pre-proto-Semitic—distantly ancestral to the much later Semitic languages—and proto-Boreafrasian. It is this second daughter language that gave rise to the ancestral line of descent out of which the ancient Egyptian language, as well as the Chadic and Amazigh ("Berber") subgroups, would subsequently evolve (fig. 5.1).[7]

As for answering the second question—where would the daughter languages of the family have been spoken at successive eras in history?—I apply the long-established set of standard tools for inferring cultural history from comparative ethnography and linguistics.[8] Two major articles by Jan Vansina, published in the 1960s,[9] set out specifically how the principles of historical reconstruction from comparative ethnography apply in African historical studies, while my own recent publications illustrate the application of the linguistic approaches, using a variety of examples from African history.[10]

Two primary principles apply in the proposing of the ancient locations of peoples, languages, and cultural features. One is the principle of fewest moves—often called, somewhat ungrammatically, the principle of least moves. To state this idea in plain terms, the history of language spread that requires the fewest—and the

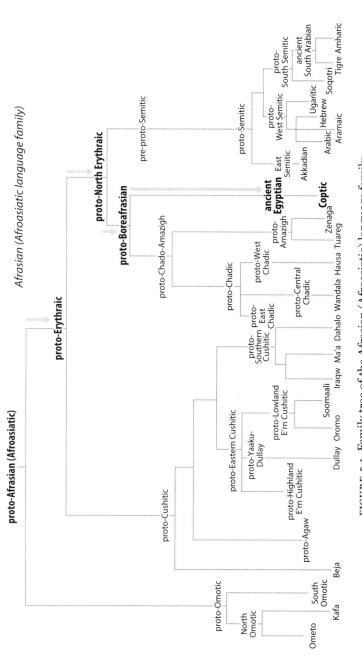

Afrasian (Afroasiatic language family)

FIGURE 5.1. Family tree of the Afrasian (Afroasiatic) language family.

most straightforward—expansions of the speakers into new lands is the most probable history. It's an application, of course, of Ockham's razor. This analytical principle is, for example, in very lively use these days among geneticists tracking the genetic origins and spreads of humankind and of particular genes. Similarly, if there is a region where the deepest branches of the language family cluster close to each other geographically, that will be the region where languages of the family have longest been spoken. The two principles, of fewest moves and greatest diversity, commonly support each other in their implications about language origins.

So how do these principles apply to the history of ancient Egyptian? The geography of the successive branchings of the Afrasian tree puts it beyond reasonable doubt, one, that the family originated in the Horn of Africa and, two, that the speakers of the languages of the family spread in a step-by-step succession of advances outward from the Horn.

The tracking of that history begins with the first two divergences of the family. As already presented in figure 5.1, the ancestral proto-Afrasian language diverged initially into two daughter languages, each ancestral to one of the two primary branches of the family: proto-Omotic, ancestral to the languages of the Omotic branch, and proto-Erythraic, ancestral to the Erythraic branch, consisting of all the rest of the languages of the family. At the second stage of Afrasian language history, this second daughter protolanguage, proto-Erythraic, then itself diverged into two daughter languages, proto-Cushitic and proto-North Erythraic— each ancestral to two further sub-branches of the family. One of these sub-branches comprises the modern-day Cushitic languages. The second sub-branch, North Erythraic, encompasses the whole remainder of the family—that is to say, ancient Egyptian; the Chadic and Amazigh language groups of the Sahel, Sahara, and Maghreb; along with the solitary subgroup of the family, Semitic, that has languages spoken outside of the African continent.

What are the historical implications of the geography of the two earliest stages of divergence in Afrasian? The Omotic

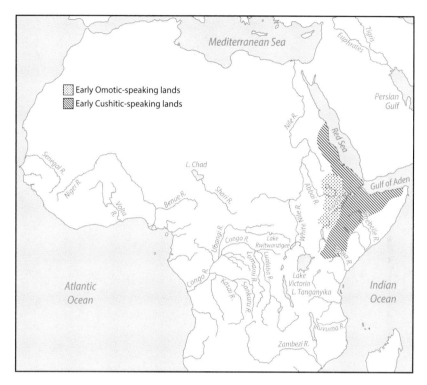

MAP 5.1. Locating the first two divergences of Afrasian: the Omotic branch and the Cushitic sub-branch of the Erythraic branch.

primary branch of the family, one offspring of the very first divergence, is entirely restricted to the Ethiopian Highlands. The second period in the divergence of the family—into two daughter languages, proto-Cushitic and proto-North Erythraic—had a comparable outcome. Once again, the languages of one of the resulting two descendant sub-branches, specifically the Cushitic sub-branch, over the long course of history came to be spoken entirely in regions in or adjacent to the Horn of Africa—lands contiguous with and extending outward from the lands of the Omotic speakers. (Map 5.1 depicts the approximate extents of the areas that peoples speaking Omotic and Cushitic languages had come to inhabit as of

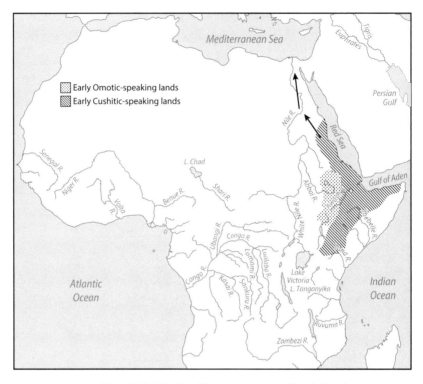

MAP 5.2. The third Afrasian divergence: proto-North Erythraic.

around 3000 BCE.)[11] The center of diversity principle thus com-
pellingly identifies the Horn of Africa as the locus of the first two
periods of divergence in the family.

Even more telling, an origin of the Afrasian family in the Horn
of Africa then allows us to account with the greatest parsimony
for *each successively later expansion* of the language family. At
the third stage in the history of the family we need postulate only
a single northward spread of the ancestral proto-North Erythraic
speakers out of the Horn toward Egypt (map 5.2).

Following that spread, just two further single expansions outward from the Egyptian corner of Africa fully account for the
locations of the remaining divisions of the family (map 5.3). The
earlier of those two further expansions involved the communities

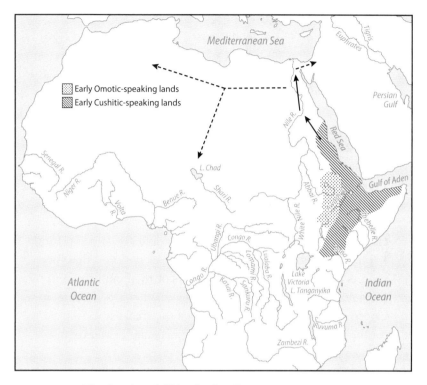

MAP 5.3. The fourth and fifth Afrasian divergences: pre-proto-Semitic and proto-Chado-Amazigh.

who spoke the particular dialect of proto-North Erythraic that would evolve, over a long span of centuries, into the much later proto-Semitic language. In linguistic terms, we would give the name "pre-proto-Semitic" to this line of language descent. A single spread of this community north out of Egypt and across Sinai accounts in straightforward manner for the proposed, much later fourth-millennium BCE location of the speakers of the proto-Semitic language in the adjacent lands of the Levant.[12] The second further expansion was that of the speakers of the protolanguage of the Chado-Amazigh group, again out of Egypt, but in this case westward across the Sahara—a population spread that accounts with similar parsimony for the later dispersals of the languages of the Chadic and Amazigh ("Berber") subgroups of the family across adjacent regions of North Africa, the central and western Sahara, and the Chad basin.

One particularly powerful set of resources then allows us to propose correlations of linguistic history with datable archaeology: the reconstructed vocabularies of material culture at each of the nodes on the Afrasian family tree. The words used in those ancient languages serve as a robust cultural archive. They tell us what the people who spoke those languages possessed, practiced, knew, and believed. If speakers of an ancient language had words for a particular thing or a particular activity, then at the very least they knew about the thing or activity connoted by those words. If we can reconstruct whole suites of words relating to particular cultural objects and activities, we know that these objects and activities were lively parts of their cultures. And if the cultural suites we reconstruct relate to material culture, we can do something else—we can search the archaeological record for the times and places where those particular clusters of material features occur.

The proto-Afrasian people, it turns out, were harvesters of wild grains. As the data in table 5.1 reveal, this economic focus continued right down through all the successive early nodes on the family tree. From at least the proto-Erythraic period they cooked their grains in the form of flat breads. The adoption of grain harvesting in northeastern Africa was most likely a response to the climate changes of Last Glacial Maximum, which peaked in the twentieth millennium BCE.[13] Widely across Africa the climates became significantly drier during this era. The effects in the Horn of Africa would have included a shrinking of forested areas and a great expansion of grassy areas, especially in the northern Ethiopian Highlands. Faced with this kind of climatic challenge, whichever society first began to harvest wild grains from the newly expanded grasslands would have gained a productivity advantage in their subsistence over other nearby foraging peoples—an advantage that would have allowed their population to grow and expand into new territories.

Table 5.1. Lexical Evidence: Harvesting of Grains in Early
Afrasian History

Proto-Afroasiatic lexicon of grain harvesting	
*maaw- / *maay-	"grain, cereal (in general)"
*tl'aayff-	"grain species (uncertain)"
*ʕeyl-	"grain prepared for eating"
*dzayj-	"(coarse?) flour"
*-xuum-	"to separate grain from chaff"
*baayn-	"grindstone"

Additional grain harvesting lexicon dating to the proto-Erythraic period	
*ḥaw-/*ḥay-	"grain (general)"
*baz-	"grain species (uncertain)"
*sowʕ-	"grain species (uncertain)"
*muš- / *miš-	"grain species (sorghum?)"
*boor-	"small grain species (uncertain)"
*buz-	"flour"
*puzn-	"flat bread"
*faʕ- or *faaʕ	"cooked grain"
*kʷ'aʔ- or *-kʷ'aaʔ-	"grain (collective plural)"
*ʕaag-	"grain plant"

Additional grain harvesting lexicon dating to the proto-North Erythraic period	
*ɣunz- or *ɣʷinz-	"grain species (pearl millet?)"
*ɬaw-	"grain (collective plural)"

So if we are to seek out archaeological correlations for the set of new economic developments revealed in the early Afrasian lexicons, there is now a salient question we need to ask: What would the diagnostic marker of this economy be? There is in fact one particular kind of item determinative of this economy, an item that survives well in archaeology, much better than the grains themselves. That item is a small, sickle-shaped stone blade with a particular surface feature diagnostic of grain harvesting: a kind of sheen caused specifically by the cutting off of many ears of grain.

In sum, we have two proposals that the combined evidence of climatology and the linguistic historical findings raise for us: that grain harvesting began in the Horn of Africa as a response to the Last Glacial Maximum, and that the earliest Afrasian speakers, who were practitioners of this kind of subsistence, lived in the Horn of Africa, probably in more northerly areas where grassland expansion would have been greatest.

How does the archaeological evidence fit with these proposals? For most of the period of several thousand years around the Glacial Maximum our archaeological knowledge of the farther northern Ethiopian Highlands is almost a blank because so few sites have yet been studied. There is one notable exception— Laga Oda—that has been excavated. It is located at the northern margin of the highlands, near the modern-day city of Dire Dawa. Both the location and the particular finds at Laga Oda fit the implications of the Afrasian lexical evidence. The occupation of this site goes back, by calibrated radiocarbon dating, to around 16,000 BCE. Already in its earliest levels one can find *the* key diagnostic item of a wild-grain-collecting economy—small blades bearing the telltale sheen of grain harvesting.[14]

How much earlier might this adaptation have emerged in the northern Ethiopian Highlands? We lack excavated archaeological sites in the region from the crucial foundational period immediately preceding 16,000 BCE, so we don't yet know how much earlier this adaptation may have begun in the Horn of Africa. But it is not at all improbable that it might go back to the high point of the Glacial Maximum, two thousand or more years before 16,000 BCE.

Most directly relevant to ancient Egyptian history, the finds at Laga Oda date to the millennium immediately *preceding* the spread of this new kind of subsistence to Egypt. In Egypt this new economic orientation arrived a thousand years later, with a calibrated dating of around 15,000 BCE. It came with the arrival of the Afian culture along the upper and middle Egyptian Nile and the closely related Qadan culture in adjacent Lower Nubia.[15] The appearance of this new economic orientation around 15,000 BCE suggests something else—that the movements of the grain-harvesting communities northward from the northern Horn of Africa to Egypt must have begun in the centuries immediately preceding 15,000 BCE. What might explain that timing?

In that particular period—between around 16,000 and 15,000 BCE—an amelioration of the extremely dry climate of the Glacial Maximum period took place. During that millennium, rainfall increased all along the Red Sea region. On the African side of the sea—in the Red Sea Hills—the increase in rainfall would have supported an expansion of grassy areas along this chain of tall hills and middling mountains between the Horn of Africa and Egypt. The emerging grasslands would have included African wild grains, such as pearl millet and other species, that the wild-grass-harvesting communities could now begin to exploit, allowing them to spread with their economy northward to Egypt.

Who were the specific people who brought this economy to Egypt at around by 15,000 BCE? The linguistic maps of the successive earliest periods of Afrasian divergence present one striking answer. One linguistic expansion in particular—the divergence of the proto-North Erythraic speakers out of the Erythraic branch of the family and their inferred move northward to Egypt via the Red Sea Hills (see map 5.2)—maps right onto the proposed routes of spread of grain-harvesting subsistence northward out of the Horn of Africa to Egypt. As previously described, two further eras of divergence within the North Erythraic sub-branch followed.

The first of these was the divergence, most probably in the next couple of thousand years after 15,000 BCE, of the proto-North Erythraic language into two daughter languages, proto-Boreafrasian and pre-proto-Semitic (see map 5.3)—the latter language being the distant but direct ancestor of the proto-Semitic language spoken thousands of years later, around 4000 BCE, in the Syria-Palestine-Israel region.[16] One archaeologically attested cultural spread in particular appears to fit in time and place with this linguistic divergence. In the middle fourteenth millennium BCE, the Mushabian culture, bringing tools and toolmaking techniques typical of late Afian and its immediate successor cultures in Egypt, became established in Sinai and the Negev. The noted archaeologist, the late Ofer Bar-Yosef, has argued that it was the merger of Mushabian with the indigenous Geometric Kebaran culture of the Levant that gave rise around 13,000 BCE to the well-studied and well-known Natufian culture of that region. This culture lasted down to the middle tenth millennium BCE and the beginnings of agriculture in the Middle East,[17] and its makers are commonly thought by scholars to have been the cultural forebears of the early Semitic speakers.

The ancestral Boreafrasian language, which would have continued to be spoken in Egypt, eventually also diverged into two lines of language descent. One gave rise to the common ancestor language, proto-Chado-Amazigh, of the Chadic and Amazigh ("Berber") subgroups of the family (see map 5.3 and fig. 5.1). The second line led down to ancient Egyptian. The initial divergence of the peoples of the Chado-Amazigh branch, westward from Egypt, can be proposed to fit in with another era of cultural spread, namely the early Holocene epoch of around 10,000 years ago. This time of climatic shift to wetter conditions allowed for the settlement, evident in the archaeology of that period, of people and their cultures once again across large parts of the northern and north-central Sahara. The communities who remained in Egypt would have spoken the language that would evolve over the next several millennia into early ancient Egyptian.

Over the whole of the long period from 15,000 BCE down to much later times, changes in particular elements of culture did take place in the lands along and around the Egyptian Nile itself and, because of changing Nile flood behaviors, changes also in the patterns of habitation and residence. But, overall, the archaeology of the Egyptian regions presents a picture of broad cultural and economic continuity extending down from the Afian period into the Holocene epoch. Wilma Wetterstrøm thirty years ago argued that this cultural continuity, in fact, lasted right through the transition from wild grain harvesting to the adoption of cultivated grains coming from the Levant, and this view continues to hold also in more recent studies. In the seventh and sixth millennia, the existing populations of Upper Egypt and, farther north, in the Fayum gradually incorporated new crops and new ways of producing them into their subsistence lives but without evidence of any notable population intrusions from the Levant into their lands.[18]

On the other hand, the initial establishment of the Afian-Qadan cultures back in the fifteenth millennium BCE surely did reflect the arrival of a new population element, namely, the people who brought wild grain harvesting to the Egyptian Nile regions. In the archaeology, their arrival introduced microliths of several new kinds, notable among them the crescent-shaped microliths for grain harvesting.

But the tool kits soon came to include, as well, carryovers of toolmaking techniques from the pre-Afian-Qadan era. What this evidence tells us is that the arrival of this new population, argued here to have spoken the proto-North Erythraic language, did not constitute a population replacement. Rather, what took place seems to have been more a reorganization and a fusion of the existing and incoming communities.

Moreover, the available genetic evidence—relating in particular to the M35/215 Y-chromosome lineage—also accords with just this kind of demographic history. This lineage had its origins broadly in the Horn of Africa and East Africa. It then spread to Egypt in the eras before farming; from there to the areas of the Levant where the pre-proto-Semitic branch of the Afrasian family was spoken; and also to North Africa and the Sahara, where it is common among Amazigh speakers in those regions.[19] The distribution partially parallels, in other words, the history of the spread of the Afrasian language family, as described here—origins in the Horn; a movement of people northward to Egypt, bringing a new demic component of Horn of Africa origin into the existing population of seventeen thousand years ago; with subsequent spreads of Afrasian speakers to the Levant and across North and Saharan Africa, bringing the same Y-chromosome lineage to the existing populations of those regions.[20]

The kind of encounter evident in the Afian period has been quite common in human history. When new people come into an area, bringing with them a set of techniques that allow them to produce more food from the same amount of land, a frequent consequence is that the existing people of the region see these new productive capacities as evidence that the new arrivals have a superior mastery of nature—and that the newcomers possess a more potent connection with the realm of spirit that lies behind nature. And so the previous inhabitants see both a material and a spiritual advantage in allying with those societies and adopting the new practices.

A typical historical consequence of this kind of encounter is for a new social formation to emerge, in which the language of the incoming people becomes the favored language of the emerging society, and a new cultural blend takes shape—one that strongly draws on the practices of the incoming people, even though still retaining culture features from the previous eras. So our very-deep-time story is not only about the movement of people from farther south in Africa bringing a new subsistence economy north to the existing inhabitants of the Egyptian Nile regions. It is a story, too, of the establishment of a new society with its language and many of its cultural ideas and practices brought in by those same immigrants.

Religion is one of the areas of culture where this kind of cultural process often plays out. The deep-time lexicon of belief among Afrasian-speaking peoples included a very old root word *netl'- that denoted a deity of some kind. By the way, the ancient Egyptian word for god, *ntr*, is a reflex of this old root word. We cannot trace this word all the way back to proto-Afrasian, but we can trace it back as far as one of the two primary daughter languages of proto-Afrasian, proto-Erythraic.[21] Because of the somewhat different usages of this word in different Afrasian-speaking societies of later ages, it is not immediately self-evident what specific kind of deity this word originally applied to. But if we turn to the comparative ethnographic evidence, we find a strong hint: One particular kind of belief system occurs *with a relict distribution* among Afrasian speakers.

First off, what is meant by a relict distribution? This is a distribution in which a particular cultural trait of long-ago origin has been preserved by people down to much later times in only a few scattered locales far separated from each other. This kind of distribution is the classic criterion for identifying an ancient item of culture—a feature that once spread uninterruptedly across wide areas, but persists in later times only in scattered, often peripheral locations—in other words, in classically *relict* locations.

In the Afrasian case, the belief system with a relict distribution was of a type called "henotheism." Henotheism is a belief system in which people accept the existence of multiple gods, but in which each local clan or group of clans, or each local population grouping of some other kind, has its own god. To receive divine protection and prosper, the community must direct its primary loyalty and ritual observances to its own god.

This kind of belief occurred in recent millennia among several far-separated groups of Afrasian-speaking peoples and nowhere in between—it has, in other words, a classic relict distribution. Among peoples speaking languages of the farthest northern branch of Afrasian, Semitic, there existed clan, tribal, or national gods, notably Yahweh of the early Hebrews, Chemosh of the Moabites, and Qos of the Edomites—all of which have long been recognized by biblical scholars as originally henotheistic in nature. I was struck long ago, as a child, by the actual wording of the first commandment of the Bible. It does not make a monotheistic claim, such as, "There is no God but Yahweh, and Moses is his prophet." Instead, to use the wording of the King James version, it makes the henotheistic claim, "Thou shalt have *no other* god *before* me" (Exod. 20:3; emphases added). The same kind of belief system also existed at the other extreme of the Afrasian map—persisting as late as the twentieth century among several Omotic-speaking peoples of far southwestern Ethiopia.[22]

And, it appears, the predynastic inhabitants of Egypt originally had this kind of belief system as well. The gods of the particular nomes (districts) of Egypt make historical sense if we understand them as the relics of a pre–Old Kingdom belief system in which each locale gave primary allegiance to its own local god. A recognition by the founding kings of the Old Kingdom of the local gods would have been a politic and surely necessary tactic for giving each nome and its inhabitants a stake in, and a sense of belonging to, the new political order. Along with those originally local gods, another category of deity of course became preeminent in the Old Kingdom—"national" gods such as Osiris, Isis, and Horus, associated with the kingship and with their powers acknowledged everywhere—giving rise to a polytheistic belief system that served to tie the society together as a whole.

The Not-So-Deep-Time Story of Egypt's Foundations, 6000–3100 BCE

And then there is the not-so-deep-time story. In the period 6000–3100 BCE the span of lands extending across the regions of modern-day Sudan, Nubia, and Upper and Middle Egypt entered into a major era of cultural reformulation.

To relate this history, I need to introduce a particular concept—the concept of a culture area. Anthropologists, as they built their discipline in the nineteenth century, encountered regions in which peoples of different historical origins had come to be involved for centuries in extensive cross-cultural encounters with each other. Because of their long histories of cultural interchange, the societies of such regions, despite their disparate earlier origins, often had come to share many features of culture with each other, and not just superficial features. They formed an interactive region of cultural interchange and cultural commonality.

Upper Egypt and the eastern Sudan belt constituted just such a zone of extensive cross-cultural influences from the sixth millennium BCE on into later millennia. In past publications I have called this long, south-north extending region the "Middle Nile Culture Area."[23] The existence of this common cultural world is now becoming the general understanding among the archaeologists who have contributed so greatly, over the past four decades, to widening and deepening our knowledge of those regions and times. The noted Egyptian archaeologist Fekri Hassan introduced this emerging perspective to a wider readership in a groundbreaking 1988 article in the *Journal of World Prehistory*.[24] Recently, in the journal *Antiquity*, David Wengrow and his coauthors bring these findings up to date. They show that what took place was the emergence, from 6000–5500 BCE onward, across that whole expanse—from a couple hundred kilometers south of the Abbai and White Nile confluence to as far north as El-Badari in Middle Egypt—of a shared complex of cultural developments—what they have called "the primary pastoral community."[25] The economy of this culture area was not wholly pastoral. A variety of evidence, both linguistic and archaeological and from human dental remains, reveals that collecting, cultivating, and harvesting of grains and other crops took place as well.[26]

Before we go any further, though, we need to understand the environmental setting of this history. Forget the idea of ancient Egypt as "the gift of the Nile." That is a conception relevant only to periods dating *after* the late fourth millennium. During the early Holocene wet phase, from the tenth millennium down to the seventh millennium BCE, the spread of vegetation and wildlife across the Sahara opened the lands away from the river to effective exploitation by wild-grain collectors and hunters, while high flood levels along the Nile had already led early in the Holocene to the abandonment, for the most part, of the areas right along the river itself.

In the nearly three-millennia period, from around 6000 to 3300 BCE, rainfall amounts decreased but still supported an environment of continuous steppe and semidesert grassland that extended, not only across middle and southern Egypt, but far south into the Sudan geographical belt. Some communities most certainly did live close to the Nile, because lesser rain amounts reduced the danger of recurrent over-high Nile floods. But the vast majority of the inhabitants of this Middle Nile Culture Area would not have lived along the river. Instead, they would have carried out their lives and their pastoral economies in the wide expanses of lands extending both west and east of the river.

As recent archaeology reveals, from 6000 BCE onward the peoples of these lands came to share much more than just a common economy. They also participated, to use Wengrow et al.'s expression, in a long-term history of "cultural convergence," with a body of common cultural ideas and ritual practices taking hold from south of the Nile confluence region northward into the later founding regions of Old Kingdom Egypt.[27] As far north as the latitude of Aswan the participants in this history of cultural interaction would have spoken languages of the Eastern Sahelian (also called "Eastern Sudanic") branch of Nilo-Saharan. From Aswan to El-Badari in Middle Egypt they spoke dialects of the language that would evolve into ancient Egyptian.

The history of cultural convergence across these lands led to the spread of common features of culture across the whole wider region. This history is notably evident in shared ceramic styles (figs. 5.2–5.4). But much more than sharings of outward material culture characterized these developments. Ritual commonalities came equally strongly to tie the whole region together. Along the river as well as far out into all the surrounding steppe grasslands—to again use the words of Wengrow and his coauthors—"treatments of the dead became remarkably uniform"; they followed "a common ritual template."[28] All across these regions, individuals were laid to rest in pits, with their knees contracted and with their hands often cupping their faces. Before burial the intact body was wrapped in animal skins or reed mats and decorated with an array of ornaments made of colored stone blades, pierced shells, and worked bone, tooth, and ivory. The peoples of these lands buried their dead, not just with the same kinds of decorative items, but also the same range of practical artifacts:

small clay, bone, or ivory vessels;
combs of bone or ivory;
stone-grinding palettes along with rubbing pebbles; and maceheads.

More often than not, the archaeology tells us, the new features of culture had their origins in the southerly areas, among people who would have spoken languages of the Eastern Sahelian ("Eastern Sudanic") sub-branch of the Nilo-Saharan family.[29] Ceramic styles, for example, evolved out of styles initiated farther south. To use the terminology of the eminent French archaeologist, Béatrix Midant-Reynes, the ceramics of the fifth and fourth millennia were "foreshadowed" in the sixth-millennium ceramics of the Nilo-Saharan-speaking areas around the confluence of the Abbai (or "Blue Nile") and White Nile Rivers.[30] The black burnished wares appear first in southern sites (see fig. 5.2 for an example from Shaheinab in Sudan), with black-and-red burnished pots and jars then becoming common both in Sudan and in Upper and Middle Egypt (see figs. 5.3 and 5.4).

FIGURE 5.2. Black burnished ware from Shaheinab, Sudan.

FIGURE 5.3. Black-and-red burnished ware
from the Badarian culture in Middle Egypt.

FIGURE 5.4. Rippled burnished ware, Qustul, fourth millennium BCE.

Maceheads (fig. 5.5), as another example, appear first in burials in Sudan in the sixth millennium, but only after that did they become a common grave good in Upper and Middle Egypt.[31] The evidence of word histories provides still another window into the material cultural influences that flowed from south to north. The words in early Egyptian for a number of important

FIGURE 5.5. Narmer macehead, ca. 3100 BCE.

features of culture came from early languages of the Eastern Sahelian sub-branch of the Nilo-Saharan family (for its placement in the Nilo-Saharan family tree, see fig. 3.3).[32]

Not surprisingly, at least one of these borrowed words evokes the south-to-north contributions to the shared ceramic styles across this set of regions:

ds   jar
          Source: early Nilo-Saharan *DoS "water pot"[33]

Other word histories reveal southern influences, not just on the pastoral economy of the wider Middle Nile Culture Area but also on crop raising:

s3   cattle byre (earlier pre–Old Kingdom Egyptian *sr*)
          Source: proto-Eastern Sahelian (proto-Eastern Sudanic) *sar

mrw "bulls"; *mry* "fighting bull"
   Source: proto-Sahelian *ma:wr "ox"
pg3 wooden bowl or trough (earlier pre–Old Kingdom
   Egyptian *pgr)
    Source: proto-Eastern Sahelian (and earlier
    proto-Sahelian) *pookur
bd   watermelon
bddw bed of melons
    Source: proto-Eastern Sahelian (and earlier
    proto-Sahelian) *bod̠
t3   beer (earlier pre–Old Kingdom Egyptian *tr*)
    Source: proto-Eastern Sahelian (and earlier
    proto-Sahelian *tɛr)

The diffusion south during this time of grain crops, ultimately of Middle Eastern origin, to Middle Egypt is well known. What is not as well recognized is something encountered in chapter 3: that during the same eras other crops were already spreading north from Sudan and the Horn of Africa to Egypt—melons, gourds, cowpeas (black-eyed peas), and the castor-oil plant are among the notable such items.

Still another and especially striking body of archaeological evidence reveals the ancient sharing of common cosmological rituals and beliefs widely across the Middle Nile Culture Area. In the middle fifth millennium BCE, Nabta Playa, 300 kilometers southwest of Aswan, had become a major ritual center with astronomically oriented megalithic arrays (figs. 5.6 and 5.7). The overall material cultural indications left behind align with the conclusion that the livestock-raising inhabitants of the wider Nabta Playa region and the builders of these monuments were Nilo-Saharan-speaking peoples.

The megalithic arrangements include a calendar circle and five notable megalithic alignments, each directed toward either the heliacal rising point or the celestial positioning—as of the

FIGURE 5.6. Calendar circle, Nabta Playa.

middle fifth to early fourth millennium BCE—of a particular stellar feature. One alignment pointed toward the heliacal rising position of Sirius; a second lined up with the rising point of the belt of Orion; while the third, fourth, and fifth alignments appear to mark the precession of the heliacal rising points of Arcturus as of the middle fifth, the late fifth, and the early fourth millennia.

Moreover, at least two of these particular orientations of the major megalithic arrays at Nabta Playa connect directly with aspects of the cosmology of Old Kingdom Egypt. Most notably, in ancient Egypt the heliacal rising of Sirius, to which one of the arrays pointed, was the key event for calibrating the yearly calendar and signaling the onset of the annual Nile flood. A second major Nabta Playa alignment, toward the belt of Orion, connects up with concerns about life and death in ancient Egypt. The belt of Orion came to be associated in ancient Egypt particularly with Osiris, the god of death, the afterlife, and resurrection—and thus the god associated with the cycles of life, the regrowth of vegetation, and the return of the Nile flood each year.[34]

FIGURE 5.7. Megalith group, Nabta Playa. The photograph on the right shows a toppled section of one of the megalithic arrays. The meter stick next to the largest stone provides an idea of the size of these partially buried megaliths. The drawing on the left depicts the original layout, as it would have appeared to a person looking at it from the right side of the scene shown in the photograph.

Above and beyond their religious significance, the megalithic arrays have notable political and cultural implications. In all likelihood Nabta Playa was already the ritual center in the fifth millennium of a polity of some kind, very possibly of the Sudanic sacral type already in existence among Nilo-Saharan peoples of that period.[35] The burials associated with the megaliths reveal a significant degree of social stratification among the adherents of the site. As well, the very existence of the astronomically oriented megalithic arrays tells us that there likely existed some sort of priestly group—people who trained in and possessed the necessary astronomical expertise and who carried out the ritual responsibilities related to that knowledge.

In the middle and second half of the fourth millennium a new growth of political scale began to take hold across the middle and northern parts of the Middle Nile Culture Area—not just in southern Upper Egypt, but also in the lands inhabited by Nilo-Saharan-speaking peoples and extending well south through Nubia. The major kingdom of the period from roughly 3500 down to as late as 3200 BCE may actually have been centered in the northern Nilo-Saharan-speaking lands, immediately south of Upper Egypt, but with its hegemony probably extending north beyond the first cataract into southern Upper Egypt. It had its capital and royal burial locations at Qustul in Lower Nubia, partway between the first and second cataracts of the Nile (map 5.4), in areas now submerged by waters of the Aswan High Dam.

Bruce Williams first began to turn a spotlight on this polity in his work four decades ago. Included among the materials found at Qustul were pictorial documents depicting victorious incursions by Qustul forces into Upper Egypt.[36] Williams's findings faced opposition at the time because of long-held assumptions of ancient Egypt as being somehow in but not of Africa.[37] But as more recent work has revealed, the Qustul state, if anything, was even more influential than Williams first proposed. From the remains at sites in what is today the Western Desert, as well as in

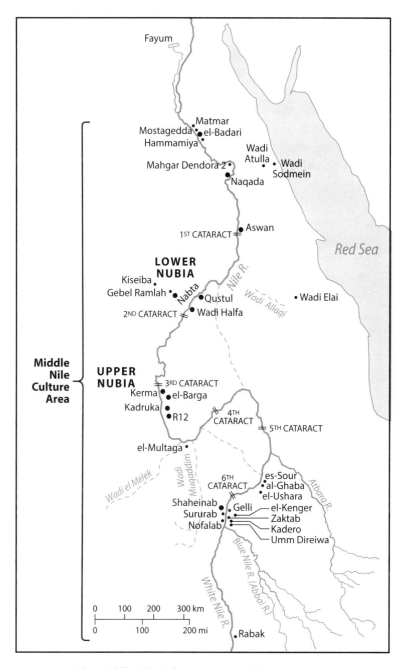

MAP 5.4. The Middle Nile Culture Area: notable archaeological sites, 5000–3100 BCE.

areas east of the Nile into today's Eastern Desert, it now appears that, in the mid-fourth millennium, the Qustul state held cultural and political hegemony over a wide expanse of lands and peoples—both along the Nile and extending outward 100–200 kilometers into the surrounding territories away from the river. The locations and layouts of the cemeteries show that this kingdom had "well developed classes," with royal and religious elites and a king with temporal and sacred power.[38]

The Qustul elites and ruler in the second half of the fourth millennium participated together with their counterparts in the communities of the Naqada culture of southern Egypt in creating the emerging culture and paraphernalia of pharaonic rule. The finds from the Qustul site include, in Williams's words, "images associated with the rising Egyptian dynastic culture," including royal symbolic facades (*serekhs*) and sacred boats. The "Qustul Incense Burner," a particularly well-studied item, "has as its primary scene a procession of three sacred boats proceeding to a *serekh* façade" (fig. 5.8). In the first boat is a bound prisoner and a guard standing behind with a mace. The ruler, who wears the White Crown, the royal headwear representative in late centuries of Upper Egypt, sits in the second boat, with the Horus falcon in front of him; while in the last boat stands a feline figure, with a falcon figure behind it, indicating that the feline figure represents a god.[39]

Then, around the thirty-fourth century BCE, a further major climatic decline took hold across these regions. Large parts of the eastern Sahara shifted over to the extremely arid climate it has today, changing much of its landscape from steppe and semidesert grassland to desert, although apparently also with remaining areas of desert grassland still able to support marginal livestock raising down to as late as around 2000 BCE. One immediate, direct consequence was the movement of pastoralists out of the emerging desert and their resettlement among the communities along the Nile itself. The Qustul kingdom, with

FIGURE 5.8. Qustul incense burner.

the falloff of its outlying populations, appears to have declined in wealth and power between 3300 and 3100 BCE.[40]

By contrast, in Upper Egypt the coincidences of timing suggest that these events set off an opposite trend during these centuries. With far more arable land along the river itself than in Lower Nubia immediately to the south, the rulers of polities in Upper Egypt controlled territories able to attract and support much greater populations, and so they would have soon been able, for instance, to field larger armies than the Qustul state could any longer put in the field.

In consequence, three notable developments came about in Egypt in the last three centuries of the fourth millennium BCE. Initially, one or more larger polities took shape in the regions of the Naqada culture in Upper and Middle Egypt. During the same time the invention of writing took place. And then, finally, in the 31st century BCE, ambitious rulers brought the First Dynasty of the Old Kingdom into being, unifying all the Nile regions from Aswan to the Delta. Hor-Aha, who was either the first or the second king of the First Dynasty, sent his forces also southward, destroying the remnants of the Qustul state and securing the southern frontier of the Old Kingdom for centuries to come.[41]

The early Old Kingdom, even with this transformation, continued to reveal the historical indebtedness of its political institutions and ritual associations to the wider Middle Nile cultural world. A particularly notable ritual practice with its origins farther south figured strongly in the early royal observances of the Old Kingdom. During the First Dynasty of Old Kingdom Egypt, the royal tombs at Abydos, it now appears, contained not just the graves of the rulers themselves, but also a large number of adjacent graves of retainers and high-status individuals, buried to accompany the king and look after him in the afterlife—36 such burials in the case of Hor-Aha and as many as 318 people in the case of his successor, Djer; 154 with the next ruler, Djet; and even 135 subsidiary graves accompanying the burial of Den, the fifth ruler.[42]

It is striking here that this ritual accompaniment of the deaths of kings similarly took place equally early farther south, and that it was a ritual feature present still in the second millennium BCE, during the high age of the Kerma kingdom of the Upper Nubian Nile region. And more than that—this ritual practice is one that historians have encountered in the histories of a number of later Nilo-Saharan-speaking, or Nilo-Saharan-influenced, states in the Sudan belt of Africa, from pre-Christian Nubia in the first half of the first millennium CE to as far west and as late in time as the Wagadu Empire of the Ghana (as the ruler was called) in the ninth century CE.[43] Egypt, viewed in the context of these wider historical developments, is best understood not as the source of this ritual practice, but as an offshoot of the Middle Nile Culture Area in which this custom took strong hold for a time, although eventually dropping out of use. But the extraordinarily deep sacredness of the royal position expressed by this kind of burial practice nevertheless persisted down into much later times, with later Egyptian kings often being called "the god."

In sum, there are two deep-time stories to relate about the Africanity of ancient Egypt. The first tracks several of the key deep roots of Egyptian culture and economy back seventeen thousand or more years ago to lands farther south, in the Horn of Africa. The second describes how the political and ritual ideas and institutions of the ancient Egyptian state and its society took shape within a wider multiethnic sphere of cultural inter-action and convergence—the Middle Nile Culture Area of the sixth through fourth millennia BCE—a cultural world encom-passing both speakers of Nilo-Saharan languages and speakers of early forms of ancient Egyptian. It now appears that, more often than not, the shared features of this common cultural sphere had their origins among those Nilo-Saharans.

Ancient Egypt's Africanity was much more than just geo-graphical. Its African cultural and political roots were primary and foundational.

CHAPTER SIX

Africa and Africans in Early Global History

CHAPTER 1 POSED THE question, how do we more fully integrate Africa and Africans into our global histories of humankind? For an answer it offered another question: What if we centered our stories on human culture and society?

This sort of approach—in giving *incidental* rather than primary attention to wars, kings, and political history—allows us to foreground the varied ways, over the long span of millennia BCE, that our human kin around the globe constructed their understandings and beliefs about their place in the world and how to deal with it. It focuses our attention on the similarly varied ways people around the world structured their social and gender relations, as well as on the separate, and often parallel, transitions they followed in their technological and material responses to the challenges they faced in different eras. For the Holocene epoch it gives central attention, moreover, to *all* the different, independent transformations of basic subsistence practices and techniques that people in distant parts of our world brought into being; to the growth of new scales of residential and political relations in many different regions of the world during the later millennia of the Holocene; and, for the last two millennia BCE in particular, to the rise of new kinds of exchange relations and to the rippling out of the social, cultural, political, and communicational consequences of those developments more and more widely across the African-Eurasian portion of world.

In the preceding chapters this kind of approach has been primary. Telling history in this fashion allows historians to bring Africa and Africans as integral actors into the overall human story of the long span of millennia BCE. What is more, this kind of approach can bring not just Africans, but the peoples of boreal Eurasia,[1] the Americas,[2] Island South Asia,[3] and Oceania[4] more fully into our overall human story.

Over the past three decades wide-ranging, new cross-disciplinary research into human cultural and social evolution has further deepened our understandings and laid the foundations for more fully integrating the *longue durée* histories of those regions as well into our telling of world history.[5] For example, the detailed reconstruction of the history of kinship vocabularies of Nilo-Saharan-speaking peoples reveals that matrilineal clans and lineages governed descent and inheritance in those societies as far back as the proto-Nilo-Saharan period, which most probably dates to the period of the Bølling-Allerød interstadials of around 12,000 to 10,000 BCE. Matrilineal descent continued to prevail among the Nilo-Saharan speakers down through the periods of their shift to pastoralism and crop cultivation in the eighth through sixth millennia BCE. This kind of descent reckoning persisted as late probably as the second and first millennia BCE among the peoples of today's Sudan and South Sudan—and is still the rule among a number those societies today.[6]

And these approaches are not something applicable just to regions late to literacy. For the regions of the world with early writing, the tools of linguistic and comparative ethnographic reconstruction, combined with those of archaeology, can add nuance and much detail to what the often-scant written records reveal about the social, cultural, and religious milieus of ancient societies. To cite just one example, in the proto-Semitic language, shown in a recent study to have been spoken in Syria-Palestine-Israel most probably around 4000–3800 BCE,[7] the word for father-in-law derived from the ancient proto-Afroasiatic word for father's brother.[8] This meaning shift is a specific identifier of the presence in a society of what is known in anthropology as "preferential parallel-cousin marriage." This particular custom reinforces paternal family solidarity, and its consistent and recurrent social accompaniment is a strongly patriarchal social structure. This word history reveals, in other words, that strong patriarchy among Semitic speakers goes back to at least 4000–3800 BCE, to an era of emerging cities along and inland from the eastern shore of the Mediterranean, but *before* the rise of large states.

As these examples from ancient kinship history suggest, it is also past time for historians, globally, to rethink gender in our recounting of the human past. Patriarchy has characterized culture and authority for several thousand years right across the whole middle belt of Eurasia, from farther East Asia to Iberia—with varying levels of subordination of women, from mild to intense, in different regions and at different eras. The discipline of written history originated in that belt of the world, and so Western history writing for a long time simply presumed men, from time immemorial, as everywhere the primary actors and shapers and women as everywhere subordinate.

The presumption that males always had authority over women profoundly affected, as well, the emerging discipline of anthropology in the later nineteenth and early twentieth centuries. It became a common anthropological interpretation that, in matrilineal societies, the father of course did not rule the extended family, but instead it was the mother's brother who did so.[9] Where the counterevidence was strong that adult women held independent authority over a broad sphere of social and cultural relations in their societies and commonly had to be consulted even in matters of war and politics—such as among the matrilineal Iroquois and Cherokee of North America and among Bantu peoples all across Africa's southern savanna belt[10]—anthropologists came to downplay or deny significance to that evidence. The anthropologist Chris Knight has written a telling account of how the historical and social milieus of the founding-era scholars of the discipline shaped and drove their retreat from the early findings about the power and agency of women in matrilineal societies.[11]

African history offers strong counterweights to these presumptions about male and female roles in history. The comparative cultural evidence across the Bantu-speaking third of Africa strongly comports with the conclusion, for example, that the authority, noted just above, of mature women in the social governance of their communities already existed during the early expansions of Bantu peoples of the third to first millennia BCE. As we have seen, women even earlier in time were the active instigators and primary participants in major material cultural changeovers in Africa, notably the inventions of ceramic technology and the creation and expansion of agricultural ways of life in large parts of the continent. Later on, from the fifth century BCE through the third century CE, the queens (Kandake)[12] of the multiethnic empire of Meroë, most of whose peoples followed matrilineal organization of kinship,[13] served as primary and powerful rulers in their own right. In much more recent times and farther south, in seventeenth-century CE Angola, in the state of Matamba—whose people also reckoned descent matrilineally—the queen, the *muhongo*, was the monarch, while her male consort commanded the state's military forces.[14]

The southern savanna belt of Africa provides a particularly notable example of the long-term historical centrality of women in the social nexus. Widely in the matrilineal societies right across those regions, a young man seeking to marry had to be approved, not by the father or even the mother's brother of the young woman he hoped to marry, but by the sororal group of her mother and her mother's female relatives. To gain their acceptance he had to perform bride service, working for months or sometimes even several years under the direction of that sororal group; and even after acceptance and marriage he was required to continue to pay an especially deep respect toward the mother-in-law. The overall distribution of these practices across an array of societies speaking languages belonging to different deep branches of the Bantu group makes it highly probable that these customs existed at least as far back in time as the proto-Savanna Bantu society of the early second millennium BCE.[15]

Widely across West Africa, whether in patrilineal or matrilineal societies, women have been from far back in the past, and continue today to be, independent social and economic actors. They have held such positions because marriage did not and does not make women in those societies economic dependents of their husbands. The major commercial entrepreneurs in recent Nigerian history, for example, have very often been women; and it turns out that women—and not just followers of the old Niger-Congo religion, but also Muslim women—were major commercial figures in that region in previous centuries as well.[16] In the trades and occupations that women carried out, they were everywhere the owners of the products of their labor. In the territories, for example, that were incorporated in the fourteenth century CE into the emerging kingdom of Benin, women were the weavers of cotton and raffia textiles, the major exports of this state even during the slave trade era, and they controlled access to their products and were prime beneficiaries of that commerce.[17]

Women, in other words, have not been always and everywhere oppressed in previous ages, and their economic, social, cultural, and, in many cases, political agency is part and parcel of the broader human history we very much need to be telling.

Global History, 68,000–20,000 BCE

Applying these various proposed perspectives leads us to distinguish, as noted previously, an initial, long historical period, from around 68,000 to 20,000 BCE. This period began with the initial emergence in eastern Africa of the fully modern human ancestors of all of us alive today. From those ancestral regions, our common ancestors then spread out, eventually around the globe, as well as across the rest of the African continent.

As previously noted in chapter 1, the defining characteristic for becoming fully modern humans, and also the primary enabling factor for this vast expansion of our common ancestors, was their acquisition of the full capacities for syntactic language, a development probably of the two or three thousand years immediately preceding 68,000 BCE.[18] This transformative shift conferred on our common ancestors the ability to build abstract interpretive structures for dealing with other people and with the world around them; to conceive of things not physically experienced and not seen; and to imaginatively build structures of meaning for coming to terms with factors beyond human control.

Verbal communication surely existed already among earlier species of the genus *Homo*. But there is a chasm of difference between the ability, likely possessed by the Neanderthals and the Denisovans and by all the various archaic hominins of Africa, to make a wide variety of communicative utterances about things seen or actions taken and the quite different ability of fully modern humans to put words, and thus ideas, together in the endless variety that the capacity for syntax allows.

Syntax is essential to being able to abstract; to classify things and experiences; and to organize one's knowledge and, from the patterns or the lack of pattern, to conceive the possibility of other things not immediately present. Possessing syntactic language allowed our first fully human ancestors to think about, and to talk with each other about, the surrounding conditions of their lives. Because fully syntactic language allows logical sorting, it allows for planning; for thinking ahead to consequences; for organizing and carrying out cooperative activities; for conceiving of novel things and novel relations among things; for categorizing, and for formulating ideas about the meaning of one's existence; and for conceiving and designing new kinds of cultural objects and, mostly notably, new kinds of technology.

Equally important, the possession of full syntactic language engendered a new scale of social cooperative abilities among our common ancestors of this age. It allowed them to conceptualize and formalize kinship and marriage relations as a basis for larger territorial groupings of bands and for structuring networks of cooperative relations among those groupings. The size of the local hunter-gatherer bands and the networks of reciprocal relations in the Later Stone Age, as this era is called in African archaeology—or Upper Paleolithic, as the same archaeological age is denominated outside of Africa—contrasts sharply with the very small size of residential groups, hardly more than small extended families among, for example, the Neanderthals.[19]

At the inception of this age, between 68,000 and 58,000 BCE, our first fully modern human ancestors, still all living in eastern Africa, brought into being two particular advances in toolmaking: the fashioning of small tools carved from bone, notably bone harpoon points, the earliest of which have been found in parts of today's Uganda,[20] and the shaping of the first small stone points and small-backed blades, found similarly early in nearby areas in Kenya and Tanzania, notably in the Mumba industry site of northern Tanzania.[21] Around 63,000 BCE this kind of toolmaking spread also to southern Africa, where it is called the Howiesons Poort culture. But while our early, fully modern ancestors in eastern Africa spread these early technological advances, over the next ten thousand years, more and more widely across eastern Africa and into the northeastern parts of the continent, in southern Africa the Howiesons Poort culture came to an end around fifty-eight thousand years ago, in the face of a reexpansion of Middle Stone Age hominins across that part of the continent. Fully modern humans finally returned permanently to southern Africa beginning from around 46,000 BCE onward.[22]

Early, fully modern humans devised, as well, the first composite projectile weaponry. Our ancestors, both those in Africa and those who began our human spread out of our home continent, participated in this history. One of the two types of early composite projectile implements was the spear-thrower (or atlatl, to use the Aztec word) and dart. Recent work identifies the first known presence of this implement among the early, fully modern humans spreading from Africa into the Levant around 48,000 BCE.[23] As people spread outward to Australia and Oceania and then across Eurasia and also, still later, to the Americas, they took this invention along with them.

In Africa itself, in contrast, the spear-thrower is not generally found—and probably for a very good reason. Recent archaeological work suggests that people living on the eastern side of Africa may have been the earliest inventors of a competing, and, ultimately, more efficient kind of composite projectile weaponry, the bow and arrow, even before fifty thousand years ago.[24] Over the long term of early world history, the bow and arrow—because it was lighter in weight, propelled its projectile at far greater speed toward its target, and was more accurate in reaching and bringing down that target—came to supplant the spear-thrower in most parts of the world.

It is the invention of these kinds of small stone blades and points, finely shaped bone points, and composite projectile weaponry that defines the emergence of the Later Stone Age in our common eastern African homeland. It is the appearance of this kind of tool kit in the archaeology that identifies the spread out of Africa of the Upper Paleolithic versions of those industries. "Upper Paleolithic," as already noted, is what the Later Stone Age is called in the archaeology of the lands outside of our home continent. The successively wider expansion in subsequent millennia of these particular kinds of tools and toolmaking advances to new regions of the world, both within Africa and outside it, serve as the definitive identifiers of the stage-by-stage advance of our fully modern ancestors outward from eastern Africa to the rest of the globe.[25]

There is a popular and widespread modern-day presumption that the bow and arrow was and somehow always has been the typical weapon of Native Americans right back through the millennia. And indeed there is some archaeological evidence for bow and arrow use early in the settlement of the Americas, but also evidence for subsequent millennia-long periods when this kind of weapon appears to have dropped out of use. The prevalence early on of the kinds of larger blades, unsuited to the arrow, such as those found in the widespread Clovis culture of 11,000 to 9000 BCE, along with the continuing use of the spear-thrower in Middle America down to recent millennia, reveal over the long term a more widespread reliance in the Americas on this type of weaponry than on archery. The bow and arrow, despite its near universality among Native Americans in very recent centuries, may finally have gained primary importance in many areas only with the arrival of new developments in the technology of archery as recently as 1,200–900 years ago.[26]

Now because the bow, bowstring, and arrow shaft are composed of eminently biodegradable materials, lasting evidence for this kind of weaponry in sites dating thousands of years ago tends to be limited to stone points that archaeological investigators can plausibly argue to have been arrowheads. So working out the fuller place of the bow and arrow across the longer term of world history will not be easy. But these are stories, because of the key place of this weaponry both in early human subsistence advances and in ancient and more recent warfare, that are well worth seeking better to understand. Exploring the histories of all the variety of tools made by our ancestors in the period leading down to twenty thousand years ago will greatly enrich the stories we can tell about the diverse cultural and material adjustments our ancestors passed through in adapting to the widely different environments they encountered as they moved out across the world.

The possession of these new kinds of technology, moreover, had two further long-range consequences. Notably, the Middle Stone Age hominins of those ages were unable to compete over the long run, eventually dying out in the face of the advance of our fully modern ancestors into new lands. Genetic studies reveal, however, that there was admixture between our modern human ancestors who emigrated from Africa and other hominins in Europe and Asia, specifically the Neanderthals and Denisovans. A further, similarly very small amount of admixture with the Denisovan hominins took place among the ancestors of the earliest fully modern human settlers of Island South Asia, New Guinea, and Melanesia.[27] Recent studies indicate that similarly small-scale interbreeding transpired also in Africa between Middle Stone hominins and those of our fully modern ancestors who expanded out of eastern Africa into other parts of our home continent.[28]

How did these encounters proceed? Was it simply the possession of the toolmaking and intellectual and language capacities that allowed fully modern humans to eventually outcompete those other hominins for subsistence resources? Or might there have been, as well, warfare and violent encounters over access to food sources? There remains much to be learned here.

Our fully modern ancestors with their new kinds of hunting technologies appear also, even in these early periods, to have gained the capacity for having a major impact on the natural world around them. Recurrently, the arrival of our human ancestors in new lands seems, in particular, to have set in motion new mass extinctions of many of the large mammals previously thriving in those places.[29] Already by 30,000 BCE in Australia, the human presence had led to the extinction of at least fourteen genera of mammals and more than eighty species of animals overall, including giant kangaroos and a huge, flightless bird, *Genyornis newtoni*.[30] Across Eurasia a similarly great set of extinctions took place, although occurring over a longer span, with such animals as the mammoth and the woolly rhinoceros able to persist down to around 10,000 years ago (and sometimes a little longer) in the peripheral, northern Siberian regions, which were settled later and more sparsely by humans. So the capacities of our species for vastly changing the world and the environment around us is not at all a development of recent history.

Notably, though, mass extinctions of megafauna did *not* take place in Africa. There, elephants, rhinos, hippos, lions, leopards, cheetahs, gorillas, Cape buffalo, and most of the vast variety of plains herbivores, from very large to very small antelopes, have persisted down to modern times. In our home continent of Africa, differently from elsewhere in the world, wild animals and our human ancestors, after all, had coevolved and coadapted to each other over the millennia—in Africa we were not an intrusive new challenge to the natural order.

Technology and material culture are not the only significant arena for fruitful future investigations into human history of the period 68,000 to 20,000 BCE. The combined fields of early religious and art history offer a striking opening for this kind of enrichment of our knowledge of those times, with developments in Africa once again integral to those stories.

Around the whole world one religious belief system occurs scattered in a conspicuously *relict* distribution across far-flung parts of the globe, from the farthest southern point of Africa to the far southern areas of South America. This kind of distribution, as described in the preceding chapter, is typical of an ancient feature of culture, once widely shared but now preserved only in scattered outlying locales. That particular religious belief system is what we might call shamanism. In this belief system existence comprises two realms, the concrete everyday realm in which we live, and the realm of spirit. The religious practitioner, the shaman, especially by going into a trance state, is believed able to connect with and even enter the realm of spirit and channel the powers of that realm into our temporal realm, to heal, harm, or foretell.[31] This religion has persisted right down to recent decades among the Khoesan-speaking peoples of southern Africa; among some societies of the Nuba Mountains region of Sudan; in a variety of societies across northern Eurasia; in native Australia; and widely among the native societies of the Americas. All in all, these global relict distributions strongly indicate than shamanism was the religion of our first fully modern ancestors even before they began to move outward from Africa.

What research has revealed over the past half century, moreover, is that the expression of this religion had deep connection to rock art around the world. Wherever we have clear evidence, it turns out to have been the shamans who were the principal artists. In this art the shamans depicted their spirit experiences, often painting or engraving figures of the animals and other items that were understood to be special links to the spirit realm. The largest of the antelopes, the eland, especially filled this role for southern African Khoesan-speaking peoples in recent millennia (fig. 6.1). Depictions in European cave art of animals such as the woolly rhinoceros seem to reflect this same sort of belief about notable animals as bearers of spirit power.[32] Engraved or painted markings, apparently symbolic, on the surfaces of objects is a practice that goes back, of course, even earlier, to our not-yet-fully-human predecessors of the later Middle Stone and Middle Paleolithic eras, as, for example, at the Blombos Cave site in South Africa[33] and among Neanderthals in Europe, as recent finds from Spain reveal.[34] But the full artistic representations of animals, plants, and people, of the kinds known from shamanistic art, seem to have originated only among our early, fully modern ancestors.

The recurrent connection of rock art and shamanism around the world has a further notable implication, namely, that the performance of rock art is likely as ancient as the religion it expresses. But because the earliest art surfaces would mostly have been open rock faces and rock shelters, the forces of wind and water would in time have entirely worn away these early artistic expressions. So far, the oldest securely dated finds of shamanistic art yet known come from caves in far separated parts of the world: Apollo Cave, for example, in Namibia in

FIGURE 6.1. Khoesan rock art, Game Pass, Kwazulu-Natal, South Africa.

southern Africa, at a bit over thirty thousand years ago;[35] numerous cave sites in southwestern Europe; and recently discovered sites in Indonesia dating as much as forty-four thousand years ago.[36] The geographical distributions, both of rock art and of shamanism, offer the prospect that we may eventually be able to find even older remnants of this kind of artistic expression.

These findings raise important further questions for historians to explore about the emergence in subsequent ages of other religious systems—systems of belief that either evolved out of, or replaced, shamanism. Major new developments in religious thought and practice do not seem to have been something engendered only as late as the great cultural and economic shifts of the Holocene epoch. As we discovered in chapter 5, for example, the comparative ethnographic evidence indicates that a different belief system, henotheism, had already emerged among the earliest speakers of the Afrasian languages, as long as twenty thousand or more years ago.

Global History, 20,000–9700 BCE

From around the height of the Last Glacial Maximum down to the beginning of the Holocene epoch around 9700 BCE, there ensued a new global age, marked by recurrent climatic challenges to our ancestors' ways of life. Around the eighteenth millennium BCE, the Last Glacial Maximum gave way to a first retreat of glaciation. But that situation did not last. With the onset of the Oldest Dryas period, colder Ice Age conditions resumed around or a bit before 16,000 BCE. Three millennia later, between around 12,700 and 10,900 BCE, a shift to warmer climate then took place during the successive Bølling and Allerød interstadials— although with a brief intervening colder period, the Older Dryas, of around 12,100 to 11,900 BCE, separating the two interstadials. A last return of Ice Age conditions came with the commencement around 10,900 BCE of the Younger Dryas period. Only with the end of this phase around 9700 BCE did the Ice Age come fully to an end, and the Holocene epoch begin.

Because of this succession of climatic reversals all around the world, the last ten millennia of the most recent Ice Age were, for our distant ancestors, a long age of back-and-forth shifts between challenge and opportunity in the pursuit of subsistence and survival. In the Glacial Maximum of the northern Ethiopian highlands, the dry climate of that period allowed local communities— shown in the preceding chapter to have been the probable early speakers of Afrasian languages—to give special place to wild grain collection in their subsistence practices. A parallel response separately took place, similarly early, 2,000 kilometers away in the Levant, with people there also beginning to take up collecting wild grains, although of quite different species from those collected in the northern Horn.

In the sixteenth millennium BCE, during the Oldest Dryas period, an opposite shift, with an increase in rainfall, took place along the Red Sea. This increase in rainfall, as described in chapter 5, would have opened an environmental corridor for the spread of wild-grain-collecting Afrasian speakers north from the Horn of Africa to Upper Egypt—a development marked in the archaeology by the arrival around 15,000 BCE of the Afian-Qadan cultural complex along the Egyptian Nile.

Elsewhere in the world another notable development marked the onset of this long historical period—the world's first invention of ceramic technology, in the Yangtze region of southern China around twenty thousand years ago. Might this development have been in some fashion a response to the subsistence challenges occasioned by the approaching end of the Glacial Maximum? Might the people of the Yangtze valley, in making this invention, have been responding to a climate-caused decline of the availability of previously common food sources and to the need to process new kinds of foods to make them more easily edible?

Still another major development of this age, probably beginning even at bit before 20,000 BCE, was the initial spread of human beings to the Americas. Because of the lowered sea levels of the Ice Age, North America and Asia joined via the lands now under the waters of the Bering Strait. Scholars often used to propose that Native American populations arrived by spreading first through interior Alaska and then, after a shrinking back of the North American glaciations later in the Ice Age, passing south via an ice-free corridor through today's Alberta. But recent scholarship has given increasing credence to an alternative proposition, that the initial Amerind expansions passed primarily along coastal areas, from eastern Siberia and Kamchatka eastward along the southern coasts of the land bridge of that age, and then southward along the western coast of North America, before spreading inland and southward to the rest of the Americas.[37] If so, the ancestral Native Americans would have been, in part, taking advantage of the availability of similar kinds of food resources across the cold northern areas, while perhaps at the same time developing an additional new subsistence reliance on resources of the seas and seashores themselves.

And as had happened previously in Eurasia, the arrival and spread of fully modern humans into these new lands similarly helped set off a series of megafaunal extinctions. During the early human settlement in North America, from around 20,000 to 10,000 years ago, a loss of thirty-five genera of mostly large animals took place, including the extinction of the ground sloth, the dire wolf, the saber cat, the American lion, horses, camels, mammoths, and mastodons. In South America, over the same broad period of initial human settlement, another fifty-two genera, including around 80 percent of all megafauna, became extinct, although a few notable animals, such as the saber-toothed cat, the giant ground sloth, and the giant armadillo may have survived for two or three millennia after 9700 BCE.[38]

Global History, 9700 to the Sixth Millennium BCE

A third big thematic period extended from around 9700 to around 5500 BCE. With the end of Younger Dryas, climate shifts ensued in many parts of the world. Those shifts brought about major changes in natural environments and, in so doing, forced peoples widely around the globe to significantly readapt their ways of obtaining food.

FROM FORAGING TO FARMING

The defining and most historically consequential response of these times, though, was the adoption of a new kind of subsistence strategy—the progressive shift over time, more and more, to the deliberate protecting and tending of particular food sources—that is to say, to the earliest *cultivation* of food plants, along, in several regions, with the protecting and herding of certain previously wild animals—with transformative long-term demographic and social consequences.

Peoples living in numerous different regions all around the globe separately and independently brought this defining new kind of economy into being between 10,000 and 6000 BCE— in Africa, Eurasia, and the Americas, as well as in interior New Guinea. The origination regions of cultivation (with early staples in parentheses) included West Africa (fonio); separately, the farther eastern Sahara regions (sorghum); and, again separately, the southwestern Ethiopian Highlands (enset, Ethiopian yams) (as described in chapter 3). Independent originating centers of agriculture in the Americas included northern Mexico (pumpkin); Central America/southern Mexico (maize, squash); highland South America (potato); northern lowland South America (sweet potatoes, peanuts, American yams); and also, although not until somewhat later, at around 5000 BCE, today's eastern central United States (sunflower, squash). Eurasian centers included northern China (foxtail millet); southern China (rice); the hill country of the "Fertile Crescent" (wheat, barley); and possibly also three areas of India.[39] Interior New Guinea (taro, banana) was still another early independent originating center of cultivation during this historical age.

In several far separated regions people also turned to the protection and herding of formerly wild animals during this era: pigs in Anatolia, and sheep, goats, and cattle in the arc of hill country west, north, and northeast around the Euphrates-Tigris lowlands; cattle separately and quite early in India; llamas in highland South America; separately, pigs in China, and, somewhat later, water buffalo in southern Asia; and donkeys in areas along the Red Sea Hills in Africa, along with the protection, and probably the early steps toward domestication, of cattle by Nilo-Saharan-speaking peoples in the eastern Sahara already by the eighth millennium BCE.[40]

Developments leading toward agriculture were not the only subsistence intensifications of this age. A particularly notable example in Africa was the rise and the extensive spread of what the archaeologist J.E.G. Sutton has called the "Aquatic Civilization of Middle Africa" or the "Aqualithic."[41] The spread in the early Holocene of the tropical African rainfall belts, with summer rain, as far north as the middle of the Sahara—coupled with the countervailing spread of the Mediterranean winter rain regime southward to the same zone—created what has often been called "the green Sahara." Rivers flowed out of the central Sahara mountain ranges of Tibesti and Hoggar, creating at least two great bodies of freshwater, Lake Fitri in today's Libya and an enormous Lake Mega-Chad, well over 600 kilometers in length, from modern-day Lake Chad in the south to the Tibesti Massif in the north. Early Nilo-Saharan speakers, advancing west, it appears, from the areas with an already aquatic economy along the Nile River, were the probable bearers of this new economy. Already in the ninth millennium BCE they would have been advancing along the new waterways and around Lake Mega-Chad, bringing with them their intensive, highly productive foraging economy, based on the catching of large fish, such as Nile perch, and on the hunting of the hippopotamus.

The mid-Holocene phase of drier climate in the later seventh and sixth millennia BCE then shifted the balance of subsistence advantage away from the Aquatic communities and toward other Nilo-Saharan speaking communities, which had long relied on dry-land food resources. During the successive proto-Northern Sudanic, proto-Saharo-Sahelian, and proto-Sahelian eras of the eighth and seventh millennia BCE (see chapter 3 and fig. 3.3), these particular Nilo-Saharans of the southern and eastern Sahara appear to have begun to protect cattle and then, over the course of the late seventh millennium, took up the full herding of cattle as well as of the newly introduced sheep and goats. At first collectors of wild grains, by the later eighth millennium, they appear—from the linguistic evidence (see fig. 3.3) and indirectly from the archaeological presence of granaries—to have begun the shift from collecting to cultivating sorghum and possibly other grains, such as pearl millet.[42]

In the sixth millennium their descendant communities were able to spread with this new economy across the Sahel and the southern Sahara as far west as the Hoggar Range and the great bend of the Niger River. The Aquatic way of life long remained viable, however, right along the streams and lakes, and the expanding pastoral Nilo-Saharan-speaking communities appear often to have assimilated Aquatic groups and their cultural and political ideas, such as sacred kingship, into their cultures.[43]

Even more notably, in two far distant African regions the evolving new ways of subsistence emerged in tandem with a major technological development, described in chapter 2, namely, two separate inventions of ceramic technology—the third- and fourth-earliest such inventions in world history. The West African inventors of the new technology utilized it from the beginning to make cooking pots. In the eastern Sahara, the earliest pottery among the Nilo-Saharan-speaking inventors of this technology included vessels for carrying water as well as for cooking food. Later, among the early mid-Holocene Nilo-Saharan herding and grain-cultivating peoples in particular, pots became important for the cooking of grains in the form of porridge.

FOOD PRODUCTION AND ITS DEMOGRAPHIC CONSEQUENCES

A common world historical feature of the increasing reliance on food production, already touched on in chapter 3, was the impetus it gave to human population growth. The growth in population soon led, in consequence, to the need for more land, while food production with its greater productivity per unit of land allowed the enlarging cultivator and also herder populations to recurrently spread more and more widely outward from their original areas.

And the spreading of people with their new forms of subsistence into new lands had a further consequence. When people in those ages expanded into new areas, their languages spread with them. In the regular course of language history, as the centuries pass, more and more changes accumulate in how those languages are spoken—in the meanings of existing words, in the adoption or coining of new words, in the grammar rules, and in the ways that people pronounce the individual sounds of the language. In this way the original language—the *protolanguage*—of the carriers of the new ways of subsistence changed, with different particular changes taking place in each of the different areas of population spread. As the changes accumulated in how the language was spoken in different regions, mutual intelligibility gradually broke down, giving rise over many centuries to an array of distinct languages all descended from that original tongue.

For the linguistically trained historian, the complexes of word histories across those languages serve as historical registers and powerful resources for recovering and depicting the *longue durée* social and cultural histories of their speakers.[44] In chapters 3 and 5, I have already considered several examples of how these kinds of histories proceeded in Africa. Two of these histories, those of the Niger-Congo family and the Nilo-Saharan family, began with the subsistence changes dating to the first four millennia of the Holocene epoch—with population expansions supported at first by advances in foraging productivity (wild-grain collection among the Niger-Congo speakers; greatly elaborated aquatic resource use among the Nilo-Saharans) and then by the gradual shift to food production (cultivation among the Niger-Congo speakers; both herding and cultivation among the Nilo-Saharan communities and their Cushitic-speaking neighbors). A third African invention of agriculture, among the Omotic-speaking peoples in far southwestern Ethiopia, began to take shape by probably around the seventh and sixth millennia BCE, with Omotic societies, over the next three millennia, spreading their enset-based farming across the breadth of the southern Ethiopian Highlands and into north-central parts of the highlands as well.[45]

Parallel trends of history played out elsewhere in the world in these eras and provide a major thematic direction to be followed up globally. The originators, for example, of the independent interior New Guinea invention of agriculture in around the eighth and seventh millennia, most probably spoke, as Andrew Pawley has argued, the proto-Trans-New Guinea language. From around 7000 BCE onward their cultural heirs spread out, introducing the new subsistence system, along with Trans-New Guinea languages, across large parts of the island and to neighboring island chains.[46] Similarly, recent scholarship gives us good reason to suppose that it was peoples speaking languages related to the North Caucasian family who, in the tenth and ninth millennia BCE, played major roles in the creation of agricultural ways of life all around the northern and northwestern parts of the Fertile Crescent. In addition, it was likely people of that background who carried the first agriculture westward across southern Europe and into interior and farther western Europe over the course of the seventh and early sixth millennia BCE.[47]

This scale of population spread has not been a phenomenon limited solely to the increase of farmers at the expense of foragers. The climatic shifts that initiated the Holocene epoch had the potential of opening up new opportunities, for example, for an expanded and more varied exploitation of wild food resources. The first wide distribution of Nilo-Saharan-speaking peoples in Africa in the ninth millennium took advantage, as we have seen, of the vastly expanded, newly available aquatic resources of the newly green Sahara.

And this kind of demographic history has not been something limited just to the Holocene. The example considered in the chapter 5—of the spread of early Afrasian-speaking people with a wild-grain-collecting economy outward from the Horn of Africa to Egypt and beyond—belongs entirely to the immediate pre-Holocene age, of the seventeenth millennium BCE onward. Wide population and cultural extensions in world history were not something that came into effect only with the adoption of agricultural practices. These examples—with Africa providing notable case studies—tell us that shifts, not only from foraging to food production, but also from one set of foraging strategies to another, can offer productive advantages that initiate population expansions into new lands.

But in the Age of Agricultural Beginnings, from the tenth to the sixth millennia BCE, this kind of population growth, in combination with the new farming and herding economies, soon would have had a further major consequence: it forever changed the relations of humans to disease. In part, the growth of human population itself, even in those times of still extremely low population densities, increased the potentials for disease transmission. But, in addition, it was an age marked by increasingly sedentary habitation patterns, with the emergence in many places of hamlets or multifamily villages, typically with nearby sites for dumping community rubbish—conditions that would have further enhanced the risk of infection by attracting potentially disease-bearing scavengers, such as rats.

Over the same eras the activities themselves of food production also opened up new pathways for disease transmission. One potential source of new diseases was the animals that people, whether in Eurasia or Africa, began to herd and to protect at night by bringing them into enclosures, either within or next to the family homestead, and thus into recurrent close contact with the human inhabitants. As well, the activities of cultivation could change the environments around farming communities in ways that opened up new possibilities for disease spread. Clearing land for cultivation in early West African agriculture appears, for example, to have led to increased areas of standing water in which *Anopheles* mosquitoes, the vectors of malaria transmission to humans, could breed in the rainy season. Because of these human activities, malaria had become, even several thousand years ago, a major disease in Africa.[48]

CULTURE AND BELIEF IN THE AGE
OF INCIPIENT AGRICULTURE

Bringing Africa fully into our conversations about world history from 9700 to 5000 has the added benefit of introducing us to new directions for broadening and rethinking our understandings of the history of ideas in the centuries from 9700 to 5000 BCE. Religion in Africa during this transitional age from foraging to farming offers two notable case studies. A common Western presumption has long been that monotheism is an idea that emerged in the past three millennia, and historians have rightly given major attention to the spread of monotheistic religions widely around the world during the most recent two millennia. But, in fact, monotheistic religions already predominated thousands of years earlier among two major groupings of African cultures and peoples—among the speakers of the Niger-Congo languages and of the Nilo-Saharan languages—long before this kind of belief emerged in the Middle East.

Among Niger-Congo-speaking peoples, aspects of whose early history were covered in chapters 2 and 3, the belief in a single Creator God goes back to probably the earliest speakers of Niger-Congo languages, proposed to have inhabited parts of Mali in around the tenth millennium BCE. The comparative cultural evidence strongly favors this conclusion, for the straightforward reason that, in recent ages, this belief was nearly universal among Niger-Congo peoples right across the continent, and *only* among Niger-Congo peoples. We cannot yet reconstruct a word for the Creator God all the way back to the proto-Niger-Congo language, but we can reconstruct a name, *Nyambe, for this Being at least as far back as the proto-South Volta-Congo language of the sixth millennium BCE—a noun that derives, fittingly, from an earlier verb meaning "to begin."[49]

The Nilo-Saharan speakers from as early as the proto-Northern Sudanic era of around the ninth millennium BCE (see fig. 3.3 for this historical node) believed in a different kind of monotheistic entity, better described perhaps not as a discrete Being but as one Spirit or Spirit Force. The anthropologists who have studied this belief system in a variety of societies have come generally to the apply the word "Divinity" to this essentially monotheistic conception.[50] The societies that follow this religion consistently use names for Divinity that identify Divinity with the sky and, by extension, with rain and often lightning. People in these societies may also invoke particular named spirits for help, but they understand such spirits to be, not distinct beings, but rather hypostases—particular manifestations—of Divinity.

The religion of Divinity provides, in addition, an example for historians of the capacity of religious systems to spread to new areas and peoples even well before the eras of long-distance commerce or written records. Early on—the overall evidence indicates the period around the seventh or sixth millennium BCE—the idea of Divinity spread from Nilo-Saharan speakers to neighboring societies in the Horn of Africa who spoke very early languages of the Cushitic branch of the Afrasian language family.[51] From the Cushitic speakers this religion then diffused subsequently to many of the Omotic-speaking peoples of the southern Ethiopian Highlands. Across all these regions the belief in Divinity widely replaced the more ancient henotheism of the earliest Afrasian-speaking peoples, except among a few Omotic societies in the farther southwestern Ethiopian Highlands (see chapter 5 for more on this earlier religion and its history).

The Age of Agricultural Exchange, 6000–3000 BCE

From around the middle of the Holocene, an emerging age of agricultural exchange began to take shape, as the expanding early agricultural systems increasingly came into contact with each other, and crops and animals began to be adopted from one system into another. In the global frame, agricultural exchange did not have a closely datable beginning or end, despite the notional dating of 6000–3000 BCE given it here. The earliest notable "exchange"—the diffusion of sheep and goats, coming from the Levant southward to Cushitic and Nilo-Saharan-speaking peoples of the eastern Sahara—began shortly before 6000 BCE. The spread in the opposite direction of a large number of crops, and one animal, the donkey, of northeastern African origin—although beginning somewhat later, between 5000 and 3000 BCE—extended more and more widely across Eurasia from 3000 BCE onward. The most important of those African contributions may have been the donkey, not only because it made possible, for the first time, the long-distance *overland* transport of trade goods and people, but because—as noted previously in chapter 3—this animal may have served as the model for the similar employment of two other animals of major long-term historical significance, the horse and the camel.

In the Americas the spread of crops from Mesoamerica, notably maize, beans, and new varieties of squash, to the old independent Native American center of domestication—the Eastern Agricultural Complex of the present-day eastern central United States—took place rather later, during the first millennium BCE. And, of course, the spread of individual domestic animals and crops to new regions of the world has continued right down to the present.

SOCIETY AND SOCIAL RELATIONS IN THE AGE OF AGRICULTURAL EXCHANGE

What gives coherence to the age of agricultural exchange was not the crop and animal exchanges in and of themselves but rather their effects on the histories of social, political, and ritual relations in different regions of the world. The adoption of new crops and domestic animals further enriched the productivity and variety of the agricultural practices of the regions they spread to. In consequence, the proportion of the diet derived from cultivation and herding progressively grew, and the proportion coming from collecting and hunting declined. The increased productivity enabled agricultural populations to continue to grow, and not just to grow in population overall, but often in the sizes and densities of the residential groupings that people lived in.

One global consequence of this age of demographic growth was the emergence of new positions of authority in many parts of the world, notably inherited ritual and political positions passed down in particular families. In Africa the distinctive type of especially sacral chiefship and kingship, present in the later fourth millennium BCE in Upper Egypt—and, from the archaeological and comparative ethnographic indications, originating centuries earlier in Nubia and the Middle Nile basin south of Egypt, a kind of kingship that continued to thrive in later ages in a wide array of states in the Sahara and Sudan belt—had its roots among Nilo-Saharan-speaking peoples. I have proposed elsewhere that this institution most probably emerged, possibly even before the middle Holocene, among the communities that exploited the aquatic resources of the "green Sahara" rather than among the herding and cultivating Nilo-Saharan speakers.[52]

In West Africa we can trace back to the proto-South Volta-Congo language of around the early sixth millennium BCE (see chapter 3 for more on this branch of the Niger-Congo peoples) the name for a different kind of inherited position, a position of clan ritual authority, the *-kumo. The comparative ethnographic evidence across a wide swath of the continent indicates that the holder of this position functioned originally as a clan ritual chief in clans of matrilineal descent, whose primary role was not as a political leader but as a spiritual intermediary in the maintaining of proper community relations with the spirits of the ancestors.[53] The holders of this position, probably quite early on, came widely to serve as moderators in communal meetings, overseeing community deliberations on the enforcement of law and custom and acting as spokespersons in intercommunity relations. In later historical eras this position often took on new powers, evolving in a number of regions into the role of political chief or king.[54]

In northeastern Africa, among peoples speaking languages of the Cushitic branch of Afrasian, a different kind of clan religious figure, the *waap'(er)-, traces back to at least the sixth millennium BCE.[55] Illustrative of the powers they were believed to wield, in some Soomaali-speaking areas of the Horn of Africa, the *waab* or *waaber* (the two forms of this old root word in different Soomaali dialects) can also be called *rooble*, "possessor of rain." Those who held this position were not political rulers per se, and never became so, but their position commanded a degree of reverence, and their opinions and views were highly influential in community decision making.

What these histories tell us is that social differentiation and political and religious elite classes were not de novo creations of the highly stratified societies that took shape by the middle of the fourth millennium BCE in several far separate parts of the world. Those stratified societies surely built their institutions on foundations laid down by earlier, smaller-scale societies— societies with emergent social status differentiations, even if of less marked and intense kinds.

By the later fourth millennium BCE a number of areas of significantly denser population concentrations had also arisen in several parts of the world. These areas included the Nile valley, both in Egypt and Nubia and, apparently, farther south in northern Sudan; Mesopotamia; the Indus valley; the two major river valleys of China; and, in the Americas, coastal Peru.[56] Historians have long seen this kind of population concentration as having major social and political consequences. An increasing inequality of access to resources and to power and status took place in those regions of more concentrated population, with, at first, social classes and chiefly levels of political authority taking shape and then, subsequently, as population and unequal access to resources continued to grow, with kings and complex social stratification emerging. A consolidation and formalization of religious authority in priesthoods commonly took place as well, sometimes in parallel with the concentration of political authority in the hands of a political elite and sometimes even before.

This kind of development had already begun, the archaeological remains indicate, in the Nilo-Saharan-speaking lands around Nabta Playa and adjacent parts of Nubia in the fifth millennium BCE. These trends came to full fruition along the Nile toward the end of the fourth millennium, when a fuller drying out of the Sahara rapidly concentrated human populations even more densely in the areas right along the river itself and, most of all, in Upper Egypt. As argued in chapter 5, the first larger territorial state may have had its center at Qustul south of Egypt proper, in the middle fourth millennium, among Nilo-Saharan speakers. The rulers at Qustul already displayed royal regalia used also by the rulers of the contemporary emerging small states of Upper Egypt and by the later rulers of Old Kingdom Egypt. The artifactual evidence indicates that the hegemony of the Qustul state at times extended south into today's Sudan; into lands as much as 200 kilometers west of the Nile; and into the areas east of the Nile as well.[57] The preceding more than two thousand years of deep cultural interconnection and convergence across all these lands should disabuse us, once and for all, of the notion that the origins of ancient Egypt were anything other than integrally embedded in African cultural history.

TECHNOLOGICAL INNOVATION IN THE
AGE OF AGRICULTURAL EXCHANGE

The age of agricultural exchange was also a global period of notable new technological developments. Histories have long tended to give primary attention to the use of metals, as we can see from the once-favored applications of terms such as Chalcolithic and Bronze Age to successive stages in the time period of the sixth through third millennia BCE.

Equally important, the period between 5500 and 3000 BCE was characterized by a striking set of parallel and independent inventions around the globe of the first loom technologies for weaving fabrics, with Africans as the earliest contributors to these advances. Most notable, as we have seen, was the weaving of cotton in Sudan by or before 5000 BCE; independently in India around a millennium later; and in South and Middle America only slightly later than that, and also quite independently. And these were not the only independent developments of weaving technology of this age of world history. The invention of silk weaving in China dates as early as the fourth millennium. People in the Middle East and Egypt probably equally early were weaving linen from the fibers of domesticated flax plants. In addition, Africans living in West Africa, far from the eastern Sudan regions, independently brought a second African invention of loom technology into being no later than the fourth millennium BCE, applying this kind of technology to the weaving of raffia cloth.

In many if not most cases it was not people who lived in states or highly stratified societies who created these various transformative technological developments. The earliest known smelting of copper from ores took place in the later sixth millennium among people living, not in Mesopotamia or the Levant or along the Nubian and Egyptian Nile, but in the Balkans. And in Africa the inventors of both cotton and raffia textile weaving lived in regions as yet without cities or states.

Nevertheless, the development of these technologies may at least in part have been stimulated by emerging social differentiation in many areas, as the growing agricultural productivity of the age of agricultural exchange allowed differential accumulations of wealth in many societies. The evidence from historical linguistics[58] gives us reason to argue that the earliest use of metals such as copper and even iron tended often to be for ornamentation as much as or more than for tools or weapons. Because of the ability of privileged people to command greater access to desired products, metal ornamentation over time tended to become an accompaniment and indicator of one's possession of wealth, status, and power.

A possible question for historians to consider is the extent to which the developments toward social stratification, in bringing about a demand for socially differentiating ornamentation, may have led over time to a greatly increased production of those metals. A growing availability, initially in Eurasia, of copper and, by the early first millennium BCE, of iron both in Africa and in Eurasia would have lowered costs and made it possible for people, more and more, to use these metals in tools and weapons and, in consequence, to turn increasingly to the rarer—and flashier—metals, such as silver and gold, as well as to copper and copper alloys, for ornamentation.

One can raise the same question about textile weaving, as a theme for historians to explore—namely, that the weaving of fabrics gained in importance, like early metallurgy, because of the demand by the higher ranks in emerging stratified societies for garments that signaled and validated their status. This possibility makes good sense for cotton use in the society of the Khartoum Neolithic of Sudan, because our evidence, although indirect, suggests the early presence of sacral chiefs among especially those Nilo-Saharan peoples who lived near major waterways, such as along the Nile itself.[59] These implications resonate with history in the Americas as well: the earliest cotton weaving belongs close in time to the rise of early political and social stratification in coastal Peru from the mid-fourth millennium BCE onward.

The age of agricultural exchange was indeed an age of agricultural expansion and elaboration and of increasing social inequalities, but it was also a time of notable technological advance. Historians have long taken note of the growing use of metals in the fifth and fourth millennia BCE. But even more strikingly expressive of human technical creativity and inventiveness, the overall period from the sixth through the fourth millennia BCE was globally the first age of textiles.

Global History, 3000 BCE–300 CE

As for the history of the last three millennia BCE and first several centuries CE, a number of major themes with wide global or regional impact stand out.

THE SPREAD OF AGRICULTURE
INTO NEW LANDS

Notably, it was in this age that agricultural ways of life spread to nearly all of the remaining areas of the earth suitable for farming. And these developments brought along with them the kinds of social, cultural, and demographic consequences that this type of transformation of subsistence supported. The long and complex histories of the spread, between 3000 BCE and 300 CE, of the speakers of languages of the Bantu subgroup of the Niger-Congo family across most of the southern third of Africa constitute the example best known to historians and most likely to receive significant coverage in a book of world history.[60]

A second major spread of the agricultural frontier, largely unrecognized, however, by historians, also took place in Africa over the last three millennia BCE. Between around 3000 and 1000 BCE, peoples speaking languages of Ubangian subgroup of the North Voltaic branch of the Niger-Congo language family (see fig. 3.2) spread through the lands immediately north of the Bantu regions of expansion. They established themselves across most of the vast basin of the Ubangi River of today's Central African Republic and the far northern parts of the Democratic Republic of Congo, with their easternmost settlements overlapping into western South Sudan by the first millennium BCE.[61] The Ubangian peoples brought with them a mixture of African crops, with yams most important in southern, wetter parts of the Ubangi basin, and with sorghum the more important crop in the drier northern parts of this zone.

During the same era in a different part of the world, communities speaking languages of the Malayo-Polynesian branch of the Austronesian family similarly spread out, first to the Philippines and, from there, across almost all of today's Indonesia as well as moving in along the north edges of New Guinea, bringing East Asian crops, notably rice, into many of these regions. These expansions had an additional set of consequences. The encounters with the existing populations of New Guinea and neighboring islands led to the adoption by the early Malayo-Polynesians of tropical crops, such as taro, breadfruit, yam, and sugarcane, several of which came from the earlier independent center of agricultural invention in New Guinea. Bringing this story into our world history gives proper credit to the inventiveness of the ancient Papuans, while again invoking a key linking factor in our human history of those times—namely, agricultural exchange and its wider consequences for society and culture.

Around 1500 BCE, there began, over the next 2,500 years, a vast additional scattering out of the speakers of the Oceanic subgroup of Malayo-Polynesian eastward into the Pacific, bringing the first agricultural, and often the first human, settlements to islands all across Micronesia and Polynesia.[62] Interestingly, the East Asian crops, notably rice, carried to Island South Asia by the initial Malayo-Polynesian expansion, did not spread with the Oceanic peoples. Rather, it was tropical crops, including those domesticated as part of the earlier independent invention of agriculture in New Guinea, that the Oceanic societies took along with them into the Pacific.

Developments in the farther northern and southern portions of the world offer still another perspective on how historical processes played out during the continuing spread of agriculture and livestock raising. Environmental differences commonly delayed the expansion of food-producing ways of life into those regions. The constraints of environment, by diverting the spread of immigrant farmers away from those regions, gave time for many of the existing inhabitants to adapt to the new possibilities by gradually incorporating food-producing activities into their previously wholly foraging economies. The histories of the Uralic speakers of the European boreal forest zone and of the Khoe peoples of southern Africa, described in chapter 3, provide salient examples of the differing paths by which people, in this kind of historical circumstance, adopted food-producing activities into their livelihoods.

The expansion of agricultural frontiers in this age was not limited to the Eastern Hemisphere. By the later first millennium BCE, the addition, described previously, of a new suite of crops from Mexico into the Eastern Agricultural Complex of today's east-central and southern United States had begun to greatly enhance the productivity of farming across those areas. With this enriched agricultural productivity, the ancestral Iroquois-Cherokee speakers expanded across lands extending from present-day Tennessee and North Carolina to southern Ontario in Canada, while early speakers of Caddoan and Siouan languages spread this economy northward through the Great Plains region of North America as far as modern-day North Dakota. In South America and the Caribbean, similar histories may lay behind the very wide spread of the Arawakan and Tupi-Guarani language groups during this age, making these still other histories much deserving of inclusion in the global human story of the last three millennia BCE.

EARLY UNEQUAL AND STRATIFIED SOCIETIES

A second recurrent theme of the age from 3000 BCE to 300 CE is a more familiar one to readers of history. It conforms to the kind of "ancient" history that scholars traditionally have given the most attention to—namely, the rise of early states and towns and of highly unequal and stratified societies. These sorts of developments took place not just, however, in the parts of the world long given favored standing by historians—regions such as Egypt,

Mesopotamia, and China. And in any case, even ancient Egyptian culture itself took shape, as we have seen, within a wider, wholly African cultural sphere, with towns and monuments not just in Upper Egypt but equally early farther south along the Nile.

In addition, parallel courses of change ensued just as early on the other side of the world, in the Norte Chico culture of coastal Peru. The early Norte Chico society took shape during the same time period as the Qustul state in Nubia and the emerging states of neighboring late predynastic Upper Egypt (see chapter 5). The beginnings of the rise of the Norte Chico society date to around 3600 BCE, with its first examples of monumental building dating to late in the millennium, contemporaneous with similar developments in Nubia and Egypt and in Mesopotamia. This society persisted down into subsequent centuries as a contemporary of Old and Middle Kingdom Egypt. Its building tradition, and especially the presence of large stone warehouses in its numerous towns, reveal the existence of an elite able to exert a centralized control over labor and valued resources, with cotton apparently being a particularly prized commodity. The architectural remains also include religious centers indicative of a strong ritual component in the governance of the society, similar to what the evidence reveals for Nubia as early as the fifth and fourth millennia BCE and in Upper Egypt by the fourth millennium.[63]

The Norte Chico people, besides being early weavers of cotton in Peru, raised a variety of food crops, including sweet potatoes, maize, beans, and squash. Maize and squash, along with some varieties of beans, originated in Middle America, so their spread to Peru once more evokes a particular theme of cultural and economic import in the world history of these times—agricultural exchange between separate, independent centers of agricultural invention, with consequences for demographic growth and, indirectly, for the kinds of social and political elaboration that the Norte Chico culture evinced.

As historians long ago took note, these early, denser populations—with social stratification, priestly control of ritual, hereditary rulers, and town formation—seem to have developed most strongly along river valleys—places that tended to have river-deposited, richer soils, along with an assured availability of water for irrigation in the midst of arid lands—areas that therefore could support population concentrations. The Norte Chico society fits this pattern, as did the societies of the Qustul state and late predynastic Egypt. The sharply greater density of settlement and the competition for resources in such areas may have helped fuel the further rise of unequal access to wealth and, in tandem, unequal access to power and influence. These regions provided, in other words, material conditions supportive of the rise of the first oppressive, highly unequal societies—and that last point, in my view, ought to be a key historical lesson to draw here.

GENDER IN COMPARATIVE HISTORY

The rise of such highly unequal societies alerts us to a related issue, to wit, the consequences of these developments for gender relations. As we have seen, the comparative ethnographic evidence from a variety of areas around the world indicates that in earlier ages, as well as in much more recent times in many regions—particularly in Africa south of the Sahara, but also among Native Americans and in Oceania—women were not necessarily subordinated to men, despite the tendencies of Westerners, among others, to assume so. Not uncommonly in such societies each sex held authority over its own, complementary sphere of social and economic activities, and the opinions of women, particularly mature women, had to be taken into account in community decision making.

So was the subordination of women a normative consequence of the emergence of social stratification in ancient societies? If one views history across the long, middle belt of Eurasia, female subordination seems indeed to have arisen early in nearly every society that developed strong social stratification. But for the world more broadly, the answer seems to be, no, not necessarily. In other world regions, notably in several parts of Africa, the rise of social and economic stratification does not seem automatically to have brought female subordination along with it. The authority of the Kandake in Meroë; the major roles of economically independent women entrepreneurs even down to recent centuries in West Africa;[64] the power and authority of queen mothers in many West and Central African kingdoms, along with other institutions for exerting female agency in such states;[65] the holding of chiefly positions by women even in kingdoms in Africa's southern savanna belt,[66] and, in the case of Matamba (see above), to be the customary monarch of a state— all these examples reinforce a point already made.

The southern savanna belt of Africa provides a particularly notable example of the long-term historical centrality of women in the social nexus. Widely in the matrilineal societies right across those regions, a young man seeking to marry had to be approved, not by the father or even the maternal uncle of the young woman he hoped to marry, but by the sororal group of her mother and her mother's sisters. To gain their acceptance he had to perform bride service, working for months or sometimes even several years under the direction of that sororal group; and even after acceptance and marriage he was required to continue to display especially deep respect toward the mother-in-law. The overall distribution of these practices across an array of societies speaking languages belonging to different deep branches of the Bantu group makes highly probable the existence of these customs at least as far back in time as the proto-Savanna Bantu society of the early second millennium BCE.[67]

What is more, this ancient historical recognition of women's proprietary spheres of authority has not been a feature solely of matrilineal societies in Africa but has often persisted in patrilineal cultures as well—for example, among the Bantu-speaking societies of the past two thousand years in the African Great Lakes region.[68] In West Africa, as already noted, independent women entrepreneurs have long been prominent in societies that spoke languages of the Niger-Congo family, whether the society was patrilineal or matrilineal, and the women in recent centuries who held this kind of economic position and influence have included Muslims as well as non-Muslims.[69] Women were able to prosper in this fashion because marriage in those parts of Africa, far back in history it appears, did not entail becoming an economic dependent of the husband.

We need to reassess women's roles in history around the world and, especially, to the extent possible, in "ancient" historical periods. How have women acted as innovators and agents of major transitions in the history of material culture? Chapters 2 and 3 provide "ancient" African examples of women as primary movers in technological and agricultural innovation. What have been the customs and institutions in different ages in different parts of the world through which women have exerted authority and taken initiative in their societies and in their own lives? The varied courses of social and economic history across Africa, as we see, offer a wide array of essential testimony on just these issues.

COMMERCIAL "REVOLUTIONS"

A fourth major theme of this age, under way in the second and first millennia BCE, was the rise of the first commercial "revolutions," with a new class of society, merchants, becoming the central facilitators of newly expanding networks of long-distance trade. As we saw in chapter 4, people living well south in Africa were initiators and major participants in these transformative shifts in economic relations. The towns of Tichit provide notable early examples of this kind of economic activity already in the second millennium BCE. By or before the beginning of the first millennium BCE a similar trend of economic development was separately in progress in the eastern Mediterranean and Levant.

A major contributing factor to expansion of long-distance commercial relations was the growing demand for metals.

Across Africa and in Eurasia the first inventions and spreads of ironworking technology particularly stimulated this kind of demand. As we have seen, Africans living well south in the African continent once again were notable instigators. As with the early origins of copper smelting, similarly with iron metallurgy, the inventors of this technology resided in smaller-scale societies and not in the regions of already emerging social stratification and political consolidation. The earliest smelters of iron, so recent findings suggest (chapter 2), lived in the middle of Africa around four thousand years ago, in a region of small villages and no states. Similarly, the people who independently invented iron metallurgy in Anatolia in the first half of the second millennium BCE inhabited politically peripheral areas, west and south of the core areas of the soon-to-emerge Hittite kingdom.

The early commercial revolutions had also a major socioeconomic consequence for our understandings of world history— they brought into being a new economic basis for towns, with the new kind of town functioning first of all as a center for the manufacture of goods for trade over distance, or as a crossroads in the transport of such goods, or as both. In those centers a new class of society, merchants, gradually took on the roles of primary buyers, sellers, and capitalizers of the transportation of goods; and, particularly in West Africa, the skilled producers of valued goods banded together to secure their productive positions in the new dispensation.

In the western and central Sudan belt of Africa, as well as separately and later in the Congo basin, the new kind of economic relations and the rise of commercial centers preceded the emergence of states. The commercial revolution in those regions grew directly out of a previous age of villages and intermediate-distance trade. Differently from what took place in the Levantine-Mediterranean world, in the African cases there had been no intervening, previous age of kingdoms and highly unequal societies. Towns and long-distance commercial relations, as we have seen, began to take shape in West Africa by early in the second millennium BCE. Political chiefdoms and kingdoms arose later, in the second half of the millennium and in the first millennium BCE,[70] and still later than that—in the first millennium and very early second millennium CE—in Central Africa.[71] Not having arisen out of a prior era of highly unequal societies and economic relations, the new kind of economy tended to take hold in a more inclusive fashion among the founding participant populations south of the Sahara.

In contrast, in the lands around and east of the eastern end of the Mediterranean Sea, states and highly stratified societies had already existed for centuries. Over time, with the rise of the new kinds of economic relations, merchants increasingly supplanted the agents of kings and priesthoods as the principal movers of long-distance trade, and skilled artisans became able to work not just for kings and priesthoods, but also to respond more directly to the widening markets for their products. Kings and their courts, rather than profiting primarily from directly monopolizing the acquisition of valued goods, instead could now thrive by imposing taxes and tolls on the trade and its profits while, at the same time, increasing the value of the trade by making themselves the protectors of commerce and the routes of travel.

By the middle of the first millennium the Garamantes, Africans of the central Sahara, had connected the trade of West Africa to that of Mediterranean. Even earlier, shipping along and across the Red Sea extended Levantine trade connections to the Horn of Africa and, in the second half of the first millennium BCE, around the Indian Ocean shores to India, with Indian merchants then expanding the trade connections still farther, to southeastern Asia and Island South Asia. Late in the first millennium BCE, overland routes spread these connections also across Central Asia to East Asia. In the same period expanding sea trade began to extend these connections far south along the eastern African coast, while far away to the west other sea links led around the west side of Europe to the tin of Cornwall and the amber of the Baltic. By no later also than the first three centuries CE, traders along the trans-Saharan routes were carrying a major new product, gold from the mines and alluvial deposits of West Africa across the Sahara to North Africa, further enhancing the consequential place of Africa for our understandings of world economic history.[72]

An additional major consequence of the new kind of trade relations, as discussed in chapter 4, with historical significance down to the present, was the eventual creation in each region of the first currencies.

COMMERCE AND EMPIRE

The first millennium BCE was marked also across Eurasia by the rise of the first empires of great geographical extent—and not only across Eurasia. Historians have long given prime attention to such realms as the Neo-Assyrian Empire of the first half of the first millennium BCE; the Persian Empire of the middle centuries of the millennium; the Empires of Alexander and his successors; the Maurya Empire in India of the late fourth to early second centuries BCE; and, of course, the Roman Empire and, far to the east, the Chinese Empire, initiated in the late third century BCE by the very short-lived Qin dynasty and consolidated by the Han dynasty over the next four centuries. What historians generally neglect to give equal attention to, however, is the parallel rise during the same age of new large states in the African continent.

The Empire of Napata-Meroë is the notable case in point. At the high period of its early conquests, between around 750 and 663 BCE, the sovereigns of this multiethnic empire of mostly Nilo-Saharan-speaking peoples held sway, from their capital at Napata on the Dongola Reach of the Nile in today's Sudan, over a larger land empire and a larger population than ancient Egypt ever did. Their realm extended north-south across 2,000 kilometers of lands, from south of the confluence of the Abbai and the White Nile through most of Egypt.

Even after the loss of its lands in Egypt proper during the second half of the 600s BCE, and the subsequent move of its capital to Meroë near modern-day Khartoum, this empire continued to be a major power for the next nine hundred years, with its territories spread across 1,200 kilometers from near Aswan in modern-day Egypt through the modern-day Gezira region of Sudan. Its hegemony extended as well over the land connections of trade between the Nile and the Red Sea, and its merchants were the suppliers of gold, ivory, rhino horn, tortoiseshell, and cotton textiles to that trade. The military forces of the Meroitic Empire successfully turned back a Roman incursion in 23 BCE, following up with devastating punitive raids into southern Egypt that led to a peace treaty with the Romans the next year. The powerful women corulers, the previously mentioned Kandakes, became fabled figures in the folklore of the eastern Roman Empire, mentioned, for example, in the Bible's New Testament in chapter 8 of the Book of Acts.

The heartlands and most of the peoples of this long-lived empire belonged to the previously described ancient Nilo-Saharan cultural world, with its religious belief in a single Divinity. Taking that historical background into account brings into immediate question the whole array of past assumptions by historians about the cultural and religious relations of ancient "Kush" to Egypt. Earlier Western scholarship tended simplistically to view the Napatan and Meroitic rulers and peoples as culturally backward imitators of Egypt. Shared elements of religious observance were interpreted as adoptions by those "backward" rulers and their peoples of ideas from the "civilized" Egyptians.

Recent scholarship indicates, on the contrary, that two kinds of cultural and political considerations predominated during these eras. On the one hand, during their conquest and rule over Egypt from around 750 BCE to the mid-600s, the Napatan kings sought to consolidate and gain acceptance of their rule over their new territories by undertaking practical measures expressive of respect and reverence toward particular Egyp-

tian gods, most notably Amun, and their key places of wor-
ship.[73] On the other hand, the peoples of the heartlands of the
Napatan-Meroitic Empire, as part of the Nilo-Saharan cultural
world, would have been followers of a religion that recognized,
not multiple gods, but one Divinity. This single Divinity could,
however, manifest itself in the form of individual named spirits,
as we have already learned. The rulers and people of Napata and
Meroë, it thus seems highly probable, would have understood
the several Egyptian deities that they did give recognition to,
not as separate gods, but as simply new and different hypostases
of Divinity.[74]

A second major African state, the archaeological and mea-
ger epigraphic sources suggest, took shape southeast of the
Napata-Meroë Empire, in the Ethiopian Highlands, and almost
as early, during the middle and second half of the first millennium BCE.[75] Its successor state in the Ethiopian Highlands, the
Empire of Aksum, is, however, far better known to historians.
Aksum was at its height from the early first millennium CE up
to the seventh century. It built its prosperity and power on its
control over access to highly valued African products, notably frankincense, myrrh, gold, and ivory, and its rulers sent its
armies across the Red Sea to conquer economically competing
areas of southern Arabia. Interestingly, like Hannibal's Cartha-
ginian army, the armies of Aksum also made use of tamed African elephants in their wars.

The beginning of this age of empires coincides in timing with
the growing complexity, as the first millennium BCE wore on,
in the variety of products and the widening geographical reach
of trading links. The various particular empires tended often
to expand across areas with already complex networks of trade
relations in place—as notably exemplified by the Neo-Assyrian
conquests in the Levant and by the Roman conquest of the lands
all around the shores of the commercially central Mediterranean
Sea—or into the major producing areas of key products of the
trade, as one sees in the case of Aksum.

And there might also be a second important enabling factor at work here. This was an age of the increasing presence and use of horses almost everywhere that the climate allowed, including as far south in Africa as the Ethiopian Highlands and the open savannas of the Sudan belt. Horses allowed the much more rapid transport of people, materiel, and messages—all factors that would have supported military campaigns and the maintenance of common governance across far wider areas than previously possible. Along the already existing overland routes of trade crossing the Sahara, horses passed as early as the middle first millennium BCE from Carthage to the western Sudan belt.[76] Most likely initially desired as prestige animals by the wealthy, horses during the later first millennium CE became the basis for the creation of cavalry forces in the emerging Sudanic states and empires of that time—notably, Wagadu ("Ghana") in West Africa.

COMMERCIAL NETWORKS AND THE SPREAD OF IDEAS, INVENTION, AND PEOPLE

Still another theme of eventual global impact began also to take shape in this age: the emergence in the first millennium BCE of religions with written scriptures—or possibly more accurately, of religion-backed, sociocultural ideologies propagated by teachers and proselytizers.[77] These included Zoroastrianism, Buddhism, Daoism, Confucianism, Judaism, and, in the first millennium CE, Christianity, Manicheism, and Hinduism—with, of course, Islam still later, in the seventh century CE.

What is often not recognized is the extent to which Africans whose ancestors spoke languages of the Afrasian language family of northeastern Africa stand out as crucial founding figures in the history of one of these new religions, Christianity. Tertullian (ca. 155–220 CE), a major contributor to early church doctrine, was born in Carthage in modern-day Tunisia, of probable Amazigh ancestry. Another noted early Christian writer of Amazigh descent was Cyprian, bishop of Carthage, who was martyred by the Romans in 258 CE. Origen, a younger contemporary of Tertullian (ca. 185–253 CE) and the most prolific and influential early Christian writer and philosopher, was Egyptian. And it was the Egyptian patriarch of Alexandria, St. Alexander, and his protégé Athanasius who were leading proponents at the Council of Nicaea in 325 in the debates that established the Christian belief in the Trinity and produced the overall statement of Christian beliefs known as the Nicene Creed. Perhaps the most influential figure of all, in the development of Western Catholic Christianity in particular, was still another African of Amazigh descent, St. Augustine, born in the fourth century CE in Hippo in what is today the country of Algeria.

How were these systems, notably Buddhism, Christianity, and, later on, Islam, able grow from regional into "world" religions?

Buddhism spread across southern Asia and to East Asia, with its routes of spread paralleling those of the expanding networks of trade. The religion of Manicheism, proclaimed by the prophet Mani in the Sassanian Empire of Persia in the middle third century, spread similarly, not just along routes of trade westward to the Roman Empire but also eastward through interior Asia as far east as China. Judaism had become established in southern Arabia in the early first millennium CE, carried by people following the land and sea routes of the Arabian Peninsula, while Christianity reached the Horn of Africa and India before the fourth century CE, spreading along the same trade routes and often introduced by merchants themselves. The Empire of Aksum became a particularly notable early area of the spread of Christianity in Africa, with its king, Ezana, converting in the fourth century CE—centuries before similar conversions took place in most of Europe—and with Coptic Christianity becoming the religion of millions of Ethiopians and Eritreans down to the present day.

In the first millennium CE as well, Hinduism spread along the evolving trade links of the Indian subcontinent into the islands of today's Indonesia. And Islam, some centuries later in time, spread to West Africa along the trans-Saharan routes and also around the Indian Ocean routes to Indonesia, more often than not specifically through the agency of merchant believers.

Both individuals and larger groups also followed these routes to seek out new lands to settle in, sometimes far from their previous homes. The resettlement at the beginning of the first millennium CE of a whole small society right across the Indian Ocean, from one side of the ocean to the other, provides the most striking case. Speaking a language of the Austronesian language family ancestral to modern-day Malagasy, this community traveled first from southern Kalimantan, most probably following the trade routes to and from India—but possibly sailing directly across the Indian Ocean, all the way to the shores of northern East Africa and, sometime later, sailing from there to Madagascar.

Their saga illustrates the historically new opportunities the expanding trade connections of that era offered not just to human resettlement but also to the very long-distance spread of new crops and domestic animals and even of notable new features of cultural life. The linguistic evidence reveals that the speakers of this ancestral Malagasy language took up residence at first along the present-day Kenyan and far northern Tanzanian coasts. From the particular Bantu-speaking societies who settled in those same areas between the first century BCE and second century CE, the ancestral Malagasy adopted the raising of sheep and cows. In return they introduced their neighbors to a major new crop, the banana, and a new domestic animal, the chicken, both brought from Island South Asia.[78] They introduced, as well, a musical instrument new to Africa, the xylophone, also of Island South Asian origin. Over the course of the first millennium CE the use of this instrument spread from society to society across the continent, eventually as far west as Mali.[79] Still later, in the sixteenth or seventeenth century, enslaved Africans brought the marimba, the Central African version of the xylophone, to the Americas.

By around the third century CE, having probably already intermarried to some extent with these neighboring communities, members of the ancestral Malagasy community then sailed farther south. Crossing the Mozambique Channel, they settled on the island of Madagascar, bringing to that island an agricultural economy that commingled African and Island South Asian crops, domestic animals, and farming practices.[80]

The growing interconnections among the various African-Eurasian long-distance trade networks in the last several centuries BCE and first few centuries CE had still one other lasting, and periodically calamitous, consequence for the longer run of global human history. These links made possible for the first time the rapid transmission of particular diseases from one distant region to another: from this age onward pandemics became a recurrent factor in the global history of us all.

For all these reasons, the rise of the several commercial revolutions of the second and first millennia BCE had central importance for the course of all of subsequent human history. They set in motion, already three thousand and more years ago, the trend toward linking up—even if indirectly and through intermediaries all along the way—more and more portions of Africa-Eurasia. The routes of trade even in the first millennium BCE had become the conduits for the spread of ideas and belief systems as well as commodities, technology, people, and, potentially, disease.

In other words, the linking up of the various commercial revolutions during the first millennium BCE and the extension of commercial contacts right across the lands and the adjoining seas of the African-Eurasian world constitute a foundational development of transformative historical consequence in the eventual linking together of all of world history. Historians often give prime credit for this outcome to the subsequent age of commercial expansion, beginning from the seventh century CE onward. But that new age of commercial expansion was historically secondary. It revitalized and, at the same time, built outward from the long-distance linkages already in place well before the end of the first millennium BCE.

The later global linkages of the seventh to the fourteenth centuries CE—when Muslim-ruled lands dominated the geographically central portions of the African-Eurasian macrocontinent—if anything deepened and widened the global salience of Africa to world history. All manner of items of lasting global significance spread along these connections, from silk, to gold, to gunpowder, to the writings of Aristotle, to religion, to pandemics. The rise of European sea trade in the fifteenth and sixteenth centuries took advantage of these myriad existing connections and, from 1492 onward, by bringing the Americas and the Pacific into these networks, made those connections and their consequences for the spread of ideas, things, people, and disease fully global—and incidentally, over time, shifted the focal crossroads of world commerce more and more from the Middle East to Atlantic Europe.

Through all these periods Africa and Africans were not off the edge of history but participants in and contributors to the major trends and transitions of each age. Events and developments in Africa were integral to the human story in all periods and deserve inclusive treatment in all our appreciations of world history.

"Civilization"

The reader may note that, in surveying these histories, I have not used the word "civilization." The stories here, and in chapters 2–5, suggest that it is past time for a critical examination of the use by historians, and by us all, of that locution.[81] To speak in concrete, material terms, what have been called civilizations were simply the earliest highly stratified and, usually, unequal and oppressive societies. The building of monuments and the production of elaborate art by those societies did not mean that their peoples were somehow smarter or more able.

What monument building actually testifies to is the existence of the concentration of wealth and power in the hands of the few. It was the centralized control of the institutions and the ideologies of power and the centralized command over the instruments of coercion that enabled kings to draft the necessary labor forces for building large monuments. It was the concentration of wealth and power that gave royalty and priesthoods the means to support professional artists and to commission their artistic works.

We can and should appreciate the human and material accomplishments of those worlds. But we gain a more balanced understanding of their cultural worlds if we call them by terms more materially and objectively descriptive of their features:

> they were early centralized and stratified societies;
> and they were early urban societies in the sense that they
>   possessed at least some towns and cities.[82]

And we ought to be as direct and unblinking in our historical evaluations of their failings as we are of oppressive societies of more recent history.

To continue to apply "civilization" in its usual fashion—with some regions viewed as having "civilization" and others as not— is to continue to convey to the readers of history, whether we mean to or not, the nineteenth- and earlier twentieth-century Western division of the peoples of the world into "civilized" versus "barbarian" or "savage." Those who do not belong to a "civilization" are thus, by default, classed as less accomplished human beings and viewed as historically peripheral. This approach tends to give short shrift to all the variety of notable developments taking place around the world in all eras—developments that fed into and contributed every bit as much to our overall human material accomplishments and to what we now are, culturally and socially as human beings.

How, in any case, in an age of growing aspiration for equity and equal justice for all people everywhere, can we still pay more time in our histories to kings, nobles, dictators, and wars than to understanding and celebrating the full range of the human experience?

In the case of Africa, we also do no service to the project of giving Africans their just historical due if we continue to plant our feet in one region of the continent and look outward from there. To privilege Egypt as the source for Africa's acquisition of some intangible and subjective value judgment called "civilization" differs hardly at all from the racialist views of the nineteenth and twentieth centuries. All one has done is plant one's feet a little farther southward—not in the Levant and Mesopotamia, or in southern Europe, but in Egypt.

To glorify Egypt and to make it *the* source for the rest of Africa of something called civilization still treats the rest of Africa as *peripheral* to world history. If we do this, we continue still to view the accomplishments of the rest of its peoples as derivative. As chapters 2–4 have revealed, in technology as well as in the great economic transitions of early world history, Africans living deep in the continent initiated and contributed to the same trajectories of change and development as peoples in other parts of the world—usually just as early, and sometimes earlier. Early Egyptian culture itself, as chapter 5 brings to light, had deep African historical roots. In the fifth and fourth millennia BCE, predynastic Egyptians became participants, as well, in a wider specifically African cultural sphere—a sphere of cross-cultural interaction and exchange that extended from well south of the Sahara in modern-day Sudan northward to Middle Egypt. The key influences that shaped the political and cultural foundations of predynastic and Old Kingdom Egypt flowed, more often than not, *northward* from the lands and peoples south of Egypt, and not the other way around. Let me repeat the concluding words of chapter 5: "Ancient Egypt's Africanity was much more than just geographical. Its African cultural and political roots were primary and foundational."

In my own writings I do use the word "civilization" except in the way that one applies the term "Western civilization"—as referring to a set of peoples and societies who share many fundamental cultural ideas and practices because their cultural worlds are rooted in a shared, more ancient historical tradition.[83] From this perspective, a "culture area" is a collection of peoples from different such civilizations who, because of centuries of cross-cultural interaction, have undergone cultural convergence by building on a mix of ideas and practices coming from those originally separate, more ancient historical backgrounds.

Looking at history through the lens of ancient, common-origin historical traditions ("civilizations") and of culture areas encourages us to be inclusive in our reach. Doing so broadens and deepens our historical understanding of humanity. Following this tack focuses our attentions on the histories of both intangible culture and material life—on the cultural experiences of peoples, both varied and shared, all around the world; on the varied and differing ways we humans have responded to those experiences across time and around the globe; and on the range of beliefs and cultural mechanisms that people, in all our human variety, have created to cope with and give meaning to their encounters with the world around them.

That, after all, is what history is about.

Considerations for Historians Reading Genetic Studies

DESPITE THE GENERAL view among biologists these days that the concept of race does not apply in explaining human variation, historians need to be aware that racialist thinking can still linger unacknowledged even in the work of geneticists. The assertion in a recent such article, for example, that there is "no sub-Saharan" component in the Egyptian population betrays an unexamined assumption that traces back to racist, early twentieth-century scholarship[1]—that there was something like a "true Negro" type, and that this pure type was represented by certain coastal West African populations.[2] The adjective "sub-Saharan" is itself the particular historically loaded term used repeatedly in earlier literature to convey that kind of racialist belief and attitude, and thus a terminology very much to be avoided.

But the Horn of Africa, of course, is also entirely south of the Sahara, and, as noted in chapter 5, scholars have already identified a genetic marker of a significant population component moving north from that region, spreading not just into Egypt, but beyond there to the Levant (where early Semitic was spoken) and across North Africa and the Sahara (among Amazigh speakers). So the assertion that there is no sub-Saharan genetic component in Egypt is nonsense.

A related problem for historians to be aware of when reading the works of geneticists is that the geneticists, when trying to correlate genetics with history, too often have relied on secondary rather than primary sources—and not just secondary sources, but often outdated, occasionally even long-outdated, publications—leading them to propose insupportable correlations between genetics and other findings. This kind of mistake remains only too common, and so historians need always to be critically aware of this possibility when consulting works from the human genetics field.

But the problem of relying on outdated sources is small potatoes compared with the truly outlandish claims made in a recent article of the usefulness of genetics in proving or disproving language relationships in several of the world's language families. Referring specifically to the Egyptian and northeastern African history covered in this book, this article claims— and this is a direct quotation from the article—"Ancestry data support . . . the exclusion of Omotic languages from the Afrasian language family."[3] Excuse me? It is linguistic evidence, not genetics, that demonstrates language relationship, and the linguistic evidence for Omotic's membership in the Afrasian family is strong and clear. It is our personal, community, societal, and regional histories—where we have lived, where we or our ancestors moved to, what groups might historically have ruled over the territories we live in, and so forth—and not our genetics that determine our home language.

The world's most widespread language family, Indo-European, and one member of that family, English, provide outstanding examples of these truths. Indo-European includes the home languages of many hundreds of millions of people, of immense genetic variety, from India to the British Isles to much of North America, as well as across the Pacific to Hawaii, New Zealand,

and Australia. Moreover, tens of millions of people in the United States, coming from all manner of backgrounds from all around the world, today use English as their first language. Genetic ancestry has nothing to do with it.

So a warning to historians—what genetics has to tell us can be quite useful, but its historical claims should always be treated with critical awareness.

NOTES

Acknowledgments

1. His groundbreaking works, applying these historical tools, include *Children of Woot: A History of the Kuba Peoples* and *How Societies Are Born: Governance in West Central Africa before 1600*, along with *Paths in the Rainforests: Toward a History of Political Tradition in Equatorial Africa* and *Évolution du royaume Rwanda des origines à 1900*.

Chapter 1. Introducing the Issues and Themes

1. Ehret, "Early Humans" and "Africa from 48,000 to 9500 BCE."

2. Manning, *A History of Humanity*. Another recent book also deserving notice is Smythe's *Africa's Past, Our Future*. The author lays out the deep African origins of us all and proceeds to the lessons of both ancient and recent African history for broadening and deepening our understanding of the worlds we and our ancestors have lived in.

3. My chapters 14 and 15 in vol. 1 of the *Cambridge World History* survey this history and the relevant sources and offer a range of possible approaches for seeking to bring African developments from 70,000 to 22,000 years ago more fully into our writing of the global human history of these ages: Ehret, "Early Humans" and "Africa from 48,000 to 9500 BCE."

4. For a recent work introducing historians and readers of history to the methods of inferring history from language evidence and how to use those methods, see C. Ehret, *History and the Testimony of Language*.

5. The classic work on ethnographic methods for history is Sapir, *Time Perspective in Aboriginal American Culture*.

6. Instructive and accessible exercises in the application of such cross-disciplinary approaches to the writing of history include, among others, Ehret and Posnansky, *The Archaeological and Linguistic Reconstruction of African History*; Vansina, *The Children of Woot* and *How Societies Are Born*; Schoenbrun, *A Green Place, a Good Place*; Peter R. Schmidt, *Historical Archaeology in Africa*; Waite, *A History of Traditional Medicine and Health Care in Precolonial Central Africa*; and Ogundiran, *The Yorùbá*.

7. Confronting these issues in world history has been basic to a variety of my own previous works, most notably *An African Classical Age*; *The Civilizations of Africa*, 2nd ed.; and my chapters in vols. 1 and 2 of the recent *Cambridge World History*. My book for general audiences, *The Civilizations of Africa*, in particular, begins each chapter by relating how African developments of the period

covered in that chapter fit into and connect with the courses of historical change outside the continent, and most chapters close with a summing up that again takes account of the wider world context.

8. The South African archaeologist Shadreck Chirikure sets out a variety of examples of how this outsider perspective has distorted our understandings of historical change within Africa and the relations of those histories to developments outside the continent in his paper "Connections between Hinterland and Coastal Southern Africa."

Chapter 2. African Firsts in the History of Technology

1. Bar-Yosef et al., "Early Pottery at 20,000 Years Ago in Xianrendong Cave, China."

2. Kuzmin, "The Paleolithic-to-Neolithic Transition and the Origin of Pottery Production in the Russian Far East."

3. Zhushchikhovskaya, *Prehistoric Pottery-Making of the Russian Far East.*

4. Huysecom et al., "The Emergence of Pottery in Africa during the 10th Millennium calBC."

5. Ehret, "Agricultural Origins"; Ehret, "Sub-Saharan Africa: Linguistics."

6. For summaries of African archaeological dates that include published dates for the early sites with this pottery tradition, see Close, "Current Research and Recent Radiocarbon Dates from Northern Africa"; Close, "Current Research and Recent Radiocarbon Dates from Northern Africa, II"; S. McIntosh and R. McIntosh, "Recent Archaeological Research and Dates from West Africa"; Wendorf and Schild, *The Prehistory of the Eastern Sahara*; Rosette, "Les plus vieilles céramiques du Sahara (préhistoire du Niger)"; see also Sutton, "The Aquatic Civilization of Middle Africa"; and Sutton, "The African Aqualithic."

7. Ehret, *A Historical-Comparative Reconstruction of Nilo-Saharan*, presents extensive data bearing on the phonological reconstruction and subclassification of this family and on the reconstruction of early Nilo-Saharan noun and verb morphology, along with an extensive dictionary of early Nilo-Saharan root words.

8. Ehret, "Nilo-Saharans and the Saharo-Sudanese Neolithic"; Ehret, "Linguistic Stratigraphies and Holocene History in Northeastern Africa."

9. Gosselain, "Technology and Style" and Saidi, *Women's Authority and Society in Early East-Central Africa*, offer informative depictions of this technology and its supportive rituals from two different regions of the continent.

10. Saidi, *Women's Authority and Society in Early East-Central Africa*, 132–33, cites an example from her field studies of this kind of ritual understanding. A senior potter told her, "A few women who were lucky become potters. If at night they dreamed of an ancestor who had been a potter, they knew they had the calling. Then each night that ancestor would teach them how to gather the clay, the ritual involved in gathering clay, and how to make and fire a pot."

11. Copper did get put to use before the development of actual metallurgy because it also exists here and there in the world in the form of "native copper," relatively pure bits of the metal embedded in ores. This kind of use took place in several areas of Africa-Eurasia. In the Americas a notable example would be the Native American makers of the Old Copper Complex of the North American Great Lakes region from six thousand years ago (see Pleger, "Old Copper and Red Ocher Social Complexity," among other sources). But the outright smelting of copper ores developed in several regions of the world only after ceramic technology became known in those areas.

12. Marie-Claude Van Grunderbeek, "Essai de délimitation chronologique de l'Age du Fer Ancien au Burundi, au Rwanda et dans la région de Grands Lacs"; Van Grunderbeek, Roche, and Doutrelepont, *Le premier age du fer au Rwanda et au Burundi*.

13. Zangato, *Les ateliers d'Ôboui*; Zangato and Holl, "On the Iron Front."

14. Ehret, "The Establishment of Iron-Working in Eastern, Central, and Southern Africa." I presented these findings first in a lecture at Columbia University in September 1974, and then again with additional findings for South Sudan, almost two decades later, at the biennial Society of Africanist Archaeologists meeting at the University of California at Los Angeles in March 1992, before finally publishing them as an article.

15. See, in particular, Ehret, "The Establishment of Iron-Working in Eastern, Central, and Southern Africa," 166–68.

16. Ehret, "The Establishment of Iron-Working in Eastern, Central, and Southern Africa."

17. Ehret, "The Establishment of Iron-Working in Eastern, Central, and Southern Africa." The arrow on map 2.6 pointing to "700 BCE" marks the initial stage of this spread of ironworking, via the early Great Lakes Bantu, to the rest of the early Mashariki Bantu communities.

18. C. Ehret, "The Establishment of Iron-Working in Eastern, Central, and Southern Africa."

19. For historical arguments on the introduction and spread of ironworking in the first millennium BCE in the Bantu areas of the northeastern equatorial rainforest, see McMaster, "Patterns of Interaction."

20. Schmidt and Avery, "Complex Iron Smelting and Prehistoric Culture in Tanzania"; Schmidt and Avery, "More Evidence for an Advanced Prehistoric Iron Technology in Africa."

21. This early African technological initiative is, by the way, another of those discoveries that have faced undue scholarly skepticism. Schmidt has recently set out the evidence all over again and taken this resistance sharply to task: Schmidt, "Science in Africa."

22. Saidi, *Women's Authority and Society in Early East-Central Africa*; Mtetwa et al., "When the Smith Is a Woman," also cite interesting exceptions from recent times in which a particular individual woman was able to become a recognized iron smith and smelter.

23. Ehret, "The Nilo-Saharan Background of Chadic," presents some of the loanword evidence supporting the identification of the pre-Chadic population region as having been speakers of languages of the Western Sahelian subgroup of the Nilo-Saharan family.

24. Holl, "Early West African Metallurgies."

25. Weise, "Governance and Ritual Sovereignty at the Niger-Benue Confluence."

26. E.g., Herbert, "Aspects of the Use of Copper in Pre-colonial West Africa"; see also Herbert, *Red Gold of Africa*.

27. Modern-day Sabi languages include Bemba, spoken widely in Zambia, along with several other languages spoken in Zambia and the far southern Democratic Republic of Congo.

28. Saidi, *Women's Authority and Society in Early East-Central Africa*, chap. 2, "Correlating Linguistics and Archaeology in East-Central African History," sets out the considerable linguistic evidence for this history of ethnic shift and its strong correlations in the archaeology of the region.

29. Stanton et al., "Morphological Diversity and Relationships in the A-Genome Cottons, *Gossypium arboreum* and *G. herbaceum*"; Palmer et al., "Archaeogenomic Evidence of Punctuated Genome Evolution in *Gossypium*."

30. Arkell, *Early Khartoum*.

31. I am indebted to the noted archaeologist of Africa, Professor Merrick Posnansky, a scholar with long experience in the archaeology of African textile production, who brought these spindle whorls to my attention and explained and tutored me in detail about their significance. It is important to note, by the way, that archaeologists who were not specialists in textile artifacts had suggested previously that all of these items might have been weights for fishing lines.

32. Kriger, "Mapping the History of Cotton Textile Production in Precolonial West Africa"; Picton and Mack, "The Classification and Distribution of Horizontal Treadle Looms in Sub-Saharan Africa." (Figure 2.3 is courtesy of Erik [HASH] Hersman.)

Chapter 3. Ancient Africa and the Export of Agricultural Innovation

1. Fuller, "Agricultural Origins and Frontiers in South Asia."

2. Smith and Yarnell, "Initial Formation of an Indigenous Crop Complex in Eastern North America."

3. For two case studies, among many, of this practice in distantly separated regions of the globe and from quite different historical periods, see Konner and Worthman, "Nursing Frequency, Gonadal Function and Birth Spacing among !Kung Hunter-Gatherers" and Tsutaya et al., "Isotopic Evidence of Breastfeeding and Weaning Practices in a Hunter-Gatherer Population during the Late/Final Jomon Period in Eastern Japan."

4. See, for example, Kelly, *The Fifth Beginning*.

5. Bramanti et al., "Genetic Discontinuity between Local Hunter-Gatherers and Central Europe's First Farmers"; Skoglund et al., "Origins and Genetic Legacy of Neolithic Farmers and Hunter-Gatherers in Europe."

6. Wetterstrøm, "Foraging and Farming in Egypt"; Rahmani, *Le Capsien typique et le Capsien supérieur*.

7. Klieman, *"The Pygmies Were Our Compass,"* provides multiple insights into this long-term history of cultural and economic interaction between the Batwa and their agricultural neighbors.

8. Ehret, "Agricultural Origins"; Ehret, "Sub-Saharan Africa: Linguistics."

9. Ehret, "Who Were the Rock Artists?"; Ehret, "Linguistic Stratigraphies and Holocene History in Northeastern Africa"; Ehret, "A Linguistic History of Cultivation and Herding in Northeastern Africa"; Ehret, "Linguistic Evidence and the Origins of Food Production in Africa."

10. "Cushitic" in this context, spelled with a capital C, has *nothing* to do with the ancient kingdom Kush, spelled with a K. The people of Kush spoke not a Cushitic language but rather Meroitic, which belonged, not to the Afrasian (Afroasiatic) language family but to the quite distinct Nilo-Saharan family. Historians and linguists unfortunately got stuck with this misleading name because of the mistaken notions of nineteenth-century scholarly investigators. And the name then got too deeply imbedded in the literature to be easily gotten rid of.

11. The United States and Canada today have significant Soomaali-American communities, and there is, of course, currently a well-known Minnesota congresswoman of that ancestry.

12. Assefa, "Omotic Peoples and the Early History of Agriculture in Southern Ethiopia," sets out the detailed case for how and when this separate agricultural world emerged first in the far southwestern corner of the Ethiopian Highlands among early Omotic speakers and then spread as the Omotic societies expanded across the high-rainfall areas of the southern half of the highlands.

13. For these sources, see, among others, chap. 6, nn. 49–52, 55, 68, 69, 73, 75, and 80.

14. Huysecom et al., "The Emergence of Pottery in Africa during the 10th Millennium calBC."

15. As argued by McMaster, "Patterns of Interaction." Ehret, *An African Classical Age*, 112, presents further lexical derivational data, supportive of McMaster's evidence and indicative of this particular use of the stone ax at least as far back as the proto-Bantu era of around 3000 BCE.

16. The roots listed here and in the next several paragraphs relating to early Niger-Congo agricultural history are the initial findings of a collaborative research project undertaken by myself and several then–graduate students at UCLA in 2010–11: Regan Buck Bardeen, Brian Cooper-Owens, Martin Deberry, Allison DePasquale, Kristen Glasgow, Tiffany Gleason, Yuan-Fe Huang, Emily Marsh, Claire Moore-Cantwell, Michelle Oberman, Willis Okech-Oyugi, and Amy Pojar. The double asterisk preceding many of the following reconstructions

denotes that, although the existence of the root word is solidly attested, the phonological representation of that root is as yet provisional. A single asterisk, in contrast, indicates that the phonology of a reconstruction is more fully established.

17. This root occurs in both the Mande and Atlantic branches as well as in the Dogon branch (Dogon *fõ*) and, far to the east, in the Ubangian subgroup of the Volta-Congo sub-sub-branch. Blench, *Archaeology and the African Past*, provides a large sample of the reflexes of this root in the Mande and Atlantic branches of the family. The Proto-Gbaya (Ubangian subgroup of North Volta-Congo) reflex of this root, *fón, shifts the meaning to "sorghum"; fonio does not grow in the wetter savanna environments in which the Gbaya peoples live; for this reflex, see Moñino, *Le Proto-Gbaya*. The alert reader of these materials may note that the English word, "fonio," for this crop is a borrowing from the Atlantic branch language, Fulani.

18. Reflexes of this root include, among others, Busa (Mande branch) *ba* "to cultivate"; Volta-Congo: Ngala (North Volta-Congo: Ubangian subgroup) *ba* "to plant seeds"; Day (North Volta-Congo: Adamawa subgroup) *va-* "to cultivate"; and Igbo (South Volta-Congo) *ba* "to dig, break up soil."

19. Reflexes of this root include, among others, Serer (Atlantic branch) *khokh* "to cultivate"; More (Volta-Congo: Gur sub-branch) *kó* "to weed, cultivate"; Edo (Volta-Congo: South Volta-Congo) *kɔ* "to plant"; and Proto-Bantu (South Volta-Congo) *kok-ud- "to clear away (vegetation)."

20. Reflexes of **kpa include, among others, Buli (Volta-Congo, Gur subgroup) *kpa* "to clear ground for new crops, hoe between growing plants"; Ngbaka and Gbanziri (Volta-Congo, Ubangian subgroup) *kpa* "to weed"; Yoruba (Volta-Congo: Benue-Kwa subgroup) *kpakpa* "cultivated field." Reflexes of **gbiɛ include Ngbaka and Gbanziri (Volta-Congo, Ubangian subgroup) *gbie* "cultivated field"; Fon (Volta-Congo, Benue-Kwa subgroup) *gbe* "to weed"; and Yoruba (Benue-Kwa) *agbɛ* "farmer." The reflexes of **pʰùkʰo, all having the meaning "cultivated field," include More *fuɣu* and Dagbani (Volta-Congo, Gur branch) *pua*; Proto-Gbaya (Volta-Congo, Ubangian subgroup) *fɔ; and Brong *vwo* and Twi (South Volta-Congo) *afuw*; this noun derives from an older verb seen in Proto-Bantu, *-pùk-, "to dig up (earth)" and Pambia (North Volta-Congo, Ubangian subgroup) *fuwu* "to hoe a field."

21. Klieman, *"The Pygmies Were Our Compass"*; Fourshey et al., *Bantu Africa*.

22. Ehret, *An African Classical Age*, sets out this complex history in detail.

23. See also Manning, *Migration in World History*, for similar perspectives on the two stages in the establishing and elaborating of agricultural ways of life.

24. For the phonological sound laws and the phonological, lexical, and grammatical innovation evidence supporting the subclassification of the Nilo-Saharan family, as depicted in the Nilo-Saharan family tree in figure 3.3, see Ehret, *A Historical-Comparative Reconstruction of Nilo-Saharan*.

25. Wendorf and Schild, "Are the Early Holocene Cattle in the Eastern Sahara Domestic or Wild?"; see also Marshall and Hildebrand, "Cattle before Crops."

26. For a presentation of the correlative lexical and archaeological data relating to these specific features, see Ehret, "Nilo-Saharans and the Saharo-Sudanese Neolithic," 104–21. The lexical evidence for the house architecture is, by the way, indirect; it consists of a reconstructed word (see fig. 3.3) for a specific kind of supporting structure for anchoring the roof of, specifically, this kind of round house to its walls.

27. Ehret, "Nilo-Saharans and the Saharo-Sudanese Neolithic"; also Ehret, *A Historical-Comparative Reconstruction of Nilo-Saharan.*

28. Stock and Gifford-Gonzales, "Genetics and African Cattle Domestication."

29. Kuper and Kröpelin, "Climate-Controlled Holocene Occupation in the Sahara."

30. The currently known botanical evidence shows the watermelon to have been well established in Egypt before the mid-second millennium BCE. The ancient Egyptian word for the crop was borrowed, however, centuries earlier from Nilo-Saharan-speaking peoples to the south of Egypt, placing the initial knowledge of the crop in Egypt much earlier than the available material remains. For an up-to-date history of the cowpea and its origin areas and spread, see Herniter, Muñoz-Amatriaín, and Close, "Genetic, Textual, and Archaeological Evidence of the Historical Global Spread of Cowpea."

31. Fuller, "Agricultural Origins and Frontiers in South Asia."

32. A separate domestication of cowpeas by southern Cushites in East Africa appears to have taken place as early as the third millennia BCE, but it was the West African variety that spread far beyond the continent: see Herniter, Muñoz-Amatriaín, and Close, "Genetic, Textual, and Archaeological Evidence of the Historical Global Spread of Cowpea."

33. Kimber, "Origins of Domesticated Sorghum and Its Early Diffusion to India and China."

34. For a groundbreaking survey and interpretive presentation of the extensive evidence relating to this topic, see Boivin and Fuller, "Shell Middens, Ships and Seeds."

35. In India this tuber is called the "Chinese potato."

36. Beja-Pereira et al., "African Origins of the Domestic Donkey"; Marshall, "Asses/Donkeys: Domestication."

37. Ehret, "A Linguistic History of Cultivation and Herding in Northeastern Africa."

38. For an overall presentation of the history of donkeys worldwide, see Mitchell, *The Donkey in Human History.*

39. From the collections of the Boston Museum of Fine Arts.

40. Anthony, *The Horse, the Wheel, and Language.*

41. Ehret, "Linguistic Stratigraphies and Holocene History in Northeastern Africa"; Ehret, "Berber Peoples in the Sahara and North Africa."

42. Ehret, "Linguistic Archaeology," esp. 126–29.

43. Ehret, "On the Antiquity of Agriculture in Ethiopia."

44. Ehret, "A Linguistic History of Cultivation and Herding in Northeastern Africa."

45. Ehret, "On the Antiquity of Agriculture in Ethiopia."

Chapter 4. Towns and Long-Distance Commerce in Ancient Africa

1. Ehret, *An African Classical Age.*

2. Holl, *Economie et société néolithique du dhar Tichitt, Mauritanie.*

3. I am grateful to Professor Augustin Holl for permission to use this photograph.

4. See in particular R. McIntosh, *Peoples of the Middle Niger.*

5. Holl, "Early West African Metallurgies."

6. R. McIntosh, *Ancient Middle Niger.*

7. Bedaux et al., *Recherches archéologiques à Dia dans le Delta intérieur du Niger (Mali).*

8. Holl, *The Land of Houlouf.*

9. S. K. McIntosh, *Beyond Chiefdoms*; S. K. McIntosh and R. McIntosh, *Prehistoric Investigations in the Region of Jenne, Mali.*

10. Ehret, "Linguistic Archaeology."

11. The collections of articles in Gatto et al., *Burials, Migration and Identity in the Ancient Sahara and Beyond*, and in Sterry and Mattingly, *Urbanisation and State Formation in the Ancient Sahara and Beyond*, offer extensive new materials on the histories of towns, commerce, and societies during this age in the Sudan belt, the Sahara, and North Africa.

12. Vansina, *Paths in the Rainforests*; Klieman, *"The Pygmies Were Our Compass."*

13. Ehret, *An African Classical Age*, 274, map 11.

14. Klieman, *"The Pygmies Were Our Compass."*

15. Vansina, "The Bells of Kings."

16. McNaughton, "The Throwing Knife in African History."

17. Vansina, *Paths in the Rainforests.*

18. Garrard, "Myth and Metrology"; also Garrard, *Akan Weights and the Gold Trade.*

Chapter 5. The Africanity of Ancient Egypt

1. Schuenemann et al., "Ancient Egyptian Mummy Genomes Suggest an Increase of Sub-Saharan African Ancestry in Post-Roman Periods."

2. For an idea of the extent of Hyksos impact in northern areas of Egypt, see Bader, "Cultural Mixing in Egyptian Archaeology."

3. See the appendix at end of this book for further commentary on the issues that can arise in the interpreting of genetic historical materials.

4. Keita, "Early Farmers from El-Badari"; see also Keita, "Studies of Ancient Crania from Northern Africa"; Keita, "Further Studies of Crania from Ancient Northern Africa"; and Zakrzewski, "Population Continuity or Population Change."

5. There is an old, *horrendously* bad name for the Afrasian (Afroasiatic) language family that unfortunately still gets used by a few scholars in Europe: Hamito-Semitic. The "Hamite" part of the name comes from the biblical name of Noah's son Ham, whom Noah cursed for inadvertently seeing his father naked. In the biblical reckoning of the descent of humankind from Noah, Ham was the ancestor most notably of the Canaanites. The first use of this term, Hamite, for certain Africans arose out of the horrific adoption by white racists of a myth—a myth of their own making, *not* biblical, to justify their enslavement of Africans—that Ham was the ancestor of Africans farther south in the continent and that God had passed Noah's curse to Ham's supposed descendants by giving them dark skins. What is still more appalling is that, even today in the twenty-first century CE, some American fundamentalist Christians continue to fall back on this myth to justify their own racism. So avoid this term like the plague!

6. The late Professor A. N. Tucker of the School of Oriental and African Studies of the University of London coined the name "Erythraic" in the 1960s, from the ancient Greek name for the Red Sea. It is an apt name for this branch of the family because the early expansions of languages belonging to the branch took place, as we will see, principally in lands along the African side of that sea.

7. Ehret, *Reconstructing Proto-Afroasiatic (Proto-Afrasian)*, sets out the detailed evidence for the deepest levels in this classification. More recent work, however, shows that the internal relationships within North Erythraic are wrongly set out in that book. The newer conclusions presented here, which place ancient Egyptian together with Chado-Amazigh, but not Semitic, in the Bore-afrasian sub-branch, are reconfirmed in the findings of a recent collaborative project: Ehret, Keita, and Brandt, "Afroasiatic Language Family and Its History." For the closer relationship of Amazigh (Berber) and Chadic to each other in a Chado-Amazigh subgroup of the family, see also Bynon, "Berber and Chadic"; and Newman, *The Classification of Chadic within Afroasiatic.*

8. More than one hundred years ago, in 1916, Edward Sapir published the classic work on these, even then already well-established, methods: Sapir, *Time Perspective in Aboriginal American Culture.*

9. Vansina, "The Use of Process Models in African History"; Vansina, "The Use of Ethnographic Data as Sources for History."

10. Notably, Ehret, *History and the Testimony of Language*; also Ehret, "Linguistic Archaeology," among other publications.

11. Assefa, "Omotic Peoples and the Early History of Agriculture in Southern Ethiopia"; Ehret, "A Linguistic History of Cultivation and Herding in North-

eastern Africa." Omotic languages today are spoken across southern Ethiopia, but the occurrence of Omotic loanwords in the Agaw languages of northern Ethiopia reveals the presence, prior to 2000 BCE, of Omotic languages in those regions also.

12. On this last point see, in particular, Kitchen et al., "Bayesian Phylogenetic Analysis of Semitic Languages Identifies an Early Bronze Age Origin of Semitic in the Near East."

13. Ehret, "Africa from 48,000 to 9500 BCE"; Ehret, Keita, and Brandt, "Afroasiatic Language Family and Its History."

14. Clark and Williams, "Recent Archaeological Research in Southeastern Ethiopia (1974–1975)"; Clark and Prince, "Use-Wear in Later Stone Age Microliths from Laga Oda, Haraghi, Ethiopia and Possible Functional Interpretations."

15. Shiner, "The Cataract Tradition"; also Wendorf and Schild, *Prehistory of the Nile Valley.*

16. Kitchen et al., "Bayesian Phylogenetic Analysis of Semitic Languages Identifies an Early Bronze Age Origin of Semitic in the Near East."

17. Bar-Yosef, "Pleistocene Connexions between Africa and Southwest Asia." Olszewski, "Issues in the Levantine Epipaleolithic," argues that the microburin technique was separately present in areas east of the Jordan River from as much as seven thousand years earlier. But if so, it did not apparently have any immediate effect on toolmaking west of the Jordan, whereas the arrival of the Mushabian does seem to have had that kind of consequence. This work also does not take account of the fact that the microburin technique had also already been applied farther south in Upper Egypt in the Silsilian culture of the period 17,000–15,000 BCE and subsequently became part of the Afian and later Egyptian tool kits.

18. Wetterstrøm, "Foraging and Farming in Egypt"; Wengrow et al., "Cultural Convergence in the Neolithic of the Nile Valley."

19. Ehret, Keita, and Newman, "The Origins of Afroasiatic": "The geography of the Y-chromosome M35/215 (or 215/M35) *lineage*, which is of Horn/East African origin, is largely concordant with the range of Afroasiatic. . . . The distributions of the Afroasiatic subfamilies and this lineage can best be explained by invoking movements that occurred *before* the emergence of food production as well as after." For a detailed critical analysis of the primary evidence, see Keita, "History in the Interpretation of the Pattern of p49a,f TaqI RFLP Y-Chromosome Variation in Egypt."

20. Historians need unfortunately to be critically alert when making use of geneticists' findings, because geneticists have in the past not always been careful in using or understanding scholarship from fields other than their own. For some instructive examples, see the appendix.

21. The reflexes of this old Afrasian root word *netl'- include Arabic *nas. amat* "idol" (stem *nas.*- plus *m and *t noun suffixes; proto-Afrasian *tl' became *s. in proto-Semitic and Arabic) and proto-Southern Cushitic *netl'- "spirit, deity," along with ancient Egyptian *ntr* (root *nt*- plus old Afrasian noun

suffix *l, which regularly changed to Egyptian *r* in word-final position). See Ehret, *Reconstructing Proto-Afroasiatic (Proto-Afrasian)*, for these sound correspondences.

22. Nicolas, "The Dizzu of Southwest Ethiopia: An Essay in Cultural History Based on Religious Interactions."

23. Most recently, Ehret, *The Civilizations of Africa*, 138–40.

24. Hassan, "The Predynastic of Egypt."

25. Wengrow et al., "Cultural Convergence in the Neolithic of the Nile Valley."

26. For a recent study including human dental evidence for grain eating, see Madella et al., "Microbotanical Evidence of Domestic Cereals in Africa 7000 Years Ago."

27. Wengrow et al., "Cultural Convergence in the Neolithic of the Nile Valley."

28. Wengrow et al., "Cultural Convergence in the Neolithic of the Nile Valley," esp. 104–7.

29. Modern-day languages of that sub-branch include Dongolawi Nubian, spoken today along the Nubian stretches of the Nile in Sudan, as well as other notable languages, such as Dinka and Nuer spoken in South Sudan, and the Kalenjin and Maasai languages spoken still farther south, in Kenya and Tanzania.

30. Midant-Reynes, *The Prehistory of Egypt*, 154 and also 127–28.

31. Wengrow et al., "Cultural Convergence in the Neolithic of the Nile Valley," 105; Krzyz'aniak, "Early Farming in the Middle Nile Basin."

32. Ehret, "The African Sources of Egyptian Culture and Language."

33. The use of the capital "D" indicates an uncertainty as to which particular proto-Nilo-Saharan (PNS) consonant should be reconstructed here: the currently available comparative linguistic evidence allows either the PNS implosive *d' or the regular alveolar voice stop *d. Similarly, the capital *S indicates that either of two PNS consonants *s or *s˘ (pronounced like English *sh*) are allowed by the available comparative Nilo-Saharan evidence.

34. Malville, "Astronomy at Nabta Playa, Southern Egypt"; see also Malville et al., "Astronomy of Nabta Playa."

35. Ehret, "Sudanic Civilization"

36. Williams, "The Lost Pharaohs of Nubia"; Williams, "Forebears of Menes in Nubia, Myth or Reality?"

37. E.g., Adams, "Doubts about the Lost Pharaohs."

38. Williams, "Relations between Egypt and Nubia in the Naqada Period."

39. Williams, "Relations between Egypt and Nubia in the Naqada Period," 87; also Williams, "A-Group Society in the Context of Northeastern Africa."

40. Williams, "The Lost Pharaohs of Nubia."

41. Williams, "The Lost Pharaohs of Nubia." Some scholars credit Narmer, who is known from records from just before Hor-Aha, with being the first king of the first dynasty.

42. Bestock, "The First Kings of Egypt."

43. For further reading on the history of this political ritual feature in states of the southern Sahara and the Sudan belt of Africa, see Ehret, "Sudanic Civilization."

Chapter 6. Africa and Africans in Early Global History

1. Manning, *A History of Humanity*, offers especially valuable new proposals and overviews on developments among humans living over the past thirty or more millennia in the boreal zones of our planet and breaks new ground in doing so.

2. E.g., Brown, "The Development of Agriculture in Prehistoric Mesoamerica"; Shady Solís, *La ciudad sagrada de Caral-Supe en los albores de la civilización en el Perú*.

3. Robert A. Blust, "Prehistory of the Austronesian-Speaking Peoples"; Bellwood, "The Origins and Spread of Agriculture in the Indo-Pacific Region."

4. E.g., Ross, Pawley, and Osmond, *The Lexicon of Proto Oceanic*.

5. E.g., Allen et al., *Early Human Kinship*.

6. Ehret, "Deep-Time Historical Contexts of Crow and Omaha Systems"; also Ehret, "Reconstructing Ancient Kinship in Africa."

7. Kitchen et al., "Bayesian Phylogenetic Analysis of Semitic Languages Identifies an Early Bronze Age Origin of Semitic in the Near East."

8. Ehret, "Reconstructing Ancient Kinship in Africa."

9. Knight, "Early Human Kinship Was Matrilineal."

10. Saidi, *Women's Authority and Society in Early East-Central Africa*, presents a variety of examples and cases.

11. Knight, "Early Human Kinship Was Matrilineal."

12. *Kandake* is, of course, the source of the modern-day female given name, Candace.

13. Welsby, *The Kingdom of Kush*, esp. 26.

14. Ehret, *The Civilizations of Africa*, 351.

15. Saidi, *Women's Authority and Society in Early East-Central Africa*.

16. Weise, "Women and Trade in the Nupe-Borgu Region during the Nineteenth and Twentieth Centuries."

17. Ogbomo, *When Men and Women Mattered*.

18. Manning, *A History of Humanity*, 36–43; also Ehret, "Early Humans."

19. Ehret, "Early Humans," 344–46.

20. Feathers and Migliorini, "Luminescence Dating at Katanda—A Reassessment," show that the bone tools dates in this case fall sometime in the range of 68,000 to 58,000 BCE. These finds were formerly dated to 82,000 ± 8,000 years ago, and historians should be aware that some secondary works still have not caught up with the revised dating.

21. Ambrose, "Small Things Remembered." Around 63,000 BCE tools characteristic of the Mumba industry spread also to southern Africa, where this industry has been called the Howiesons Poort culture. Howiesons Poort lasted

in those areas only to around 58,000 BCE, when it was replaced by the use of Middle Stone Age technology. Users of Later Stone Age technology returned permanently to southern Africa from around 46,000 BCE onward.

22. For an overview of these histories, see Ehret, "Africa from 48,000 to 9500 BCE."

23. Shea and Sisk, "Complex Projective Technology and *Homo sapiens* Dispersal from Africa to Western Eurasia."

24. Sisk and Shea, "The African Origin of Complex Projectile Technology."

25. See Bar-Yosef, "The Dispersal of Modern Humans in Eurasia," for a still relevant overview of this history.

26. Maschner and Mason, "The Bow and Arrow in Northern North America."

27. E.g., McCoy, Wakefield, and Akey, "Impact of Neandertal Introgressed Sequence on the Landscape of Human Gene Expression Variation"; also Browning et al., "Analysis of Human Sequence Data Reveals Two Pulses of Archaic Denisovan Admixture."

28. E.g., Hsieh et al., "Model-Based Analyses of Whole-Genome Data Reveal a Complex Evolutionary History Involving Archaic Introgression in Central African Pygmies."

29. Some scholars have proposed climate change to have been the cause, but the overall evidence makes it clear that humans were the prime movers in each of these extinctions; see Sandom et al., "Global Late Quaternary Megafauna Extinctions Linked to Human, Not Climate Change"; and van der Kaars et al., "Humans Rather Than Climate the Primary Cause of Pleistocene Megafaunal Extinction in Australia."

30. van der Kaars et al., "Humans Rather Than Climate the Primary Cause of Pleistocene Megafaunal Extinction in Australia."

31. A key contributor to recent scholarship on this topic has been J. David Lewis-Williams; for a bringing together of his southern Africa findings, see Lewis-Williams, *Seeing and Believing*; for the wider implications of this art, see Clottes and Lewis-Williams, *The Shamans of Prehistory*.

32. Jean Clottes and David Lewis-Williams, *The Shamans of Prehistory*.

33. E.g., Henshilwood, d'Errico, and Watts, "Engraved Ochres from the Middle Stone Age Levels at Blombos Cave, South Africa."

34. Hoffmann et al., "U-Th Dating of Carbonate Crusts Reveals Neandertal Origin of Iberian Cave Art." Brooks and McBrearty, in their groundbreaking article, "The Revolution That Wasn't: A New Interpretation of the Origin of Modern Human Behavior," draw attention to the emergence, as well, among hominins of the Middle Stone Age of other such trends in the direction of modern behavior, such as the making of personal decorative materials.

35. Wendt, "'Art Mobilier' from the Apollo 11 Cave, South West Africa: Africa's Oldest Dated Works of Art."

36. Aubert et al., "Pleistocene Cave Art from Sulawesi, Indonesia."

37. Manning, *A History of Humanity*, 94–102, presents a recent overview of the debates on the settlement of the Americas.

38. Galetti et al., "Ecological and Evolutionary Legacy of Megafauna Extinctions."

39. Murphy and Fuller, "Agricultural Origins and Frontiers in the Indian Subcontinent."

40. Stock and Gifford-Gonzales, "Genetics and African Cattle Domestication"; Brass, "Early North African Cattle Domestication and Its Ecological Setting."

41. Sutton in two articles, "The Aquatic Civilization of Middle Africa" and "The African Aqualithic," surveys these developments.

42. Ehret, "Linguistic Stratigraphies and Holocene History in Northeastern Africa"; also Ehret, "Nilo-Saharans and the Saharo-Sudanese Neolithic."

43. Ehret, *The Civilizations of Africa*, 76–82, presents an overall summary of how this history unfolded; see also Ehret, "Sudanic Civilization."

44. Ehret, *History and the Testimony of Language*, offers an introduction to these methods.

45. Assefa, "Omotic Peoples and the Early History of Agriculture in Southern Ethiopia."

46. Pawley, "The Chequered Career of the Trans New Guinea Hypothesis"; Pawley and Hammarström, "The Trans New Guinea Family."

47. Bengtson, "How Do You Solve a Problem like Euskera?"; Ehret, "Agricultural Origins"; also Günther et al., "Ancient Genomes Link Early Farmers from Atapuerca in Spain to Modern-Day Basques."

48. Webb, *Humanity's Burden*, offers a sweeping history of this disease and its origins and effects.

49. Ehret, *The Civilizations of Africa*, 68.

50. For a key early study of this belief system, see Lienhardt, *Divinity and Experience*.

51. See chapter 5 and figure 5.1 for the placement of the Cushitic languages in the Afrasian (Afroasiatic) family.

52. Ehret, "Sudanic Civilization."

53. Ehret, *The Civilizations of Africa*, 63–64, 68.

54. Examples include Bantu-speaking societies in the southern savanna belt of Africa, where the word has come to denote the ruler of a chiefdom. In West Africa, in the Nupe kingdom of precolonial Nigeria, this ancient root word took on the meaning "king." The Nupe reflex of this root, *etsu*, provides a striking example of the intricacies of internal change in language histories. The form of the word in Nupe consists of a no-longer-productive noun class prefix e- added to what remains of the root of the word, -*tsu*. What happened was that, in the Nupe subgroup, the old Niger-Congo consonant-vowel sequence *ku changed, by a regular sound change law, to *tsu*. Another example of this regular sound change can be seen in the Nupe word *tsu* "to die" from the old proto-Niger-Congo root, *ku "to die." A second early sound law in the Nupe group of languages regularly deleted the last syllable of a two-or-more syllable word, removing original final -*mo* from earlier *etsumo and leaving behind just *etsu*.

55. This root word reconstructs back to the proto-East-South Cushitic node in the Cushitic branch of the Afrasian family. For the dating of that period, see Ehret, "A Linguistic History of Cultivation and Herding in Northeastern Africa."

56. Shady Solís, *La ciudad sagrada de Caral-Supe en los albores de la civilización en el Perú.*

57. Williams, "Relations between Egypt and Nubia in the Naqada Period"; also Williams, "A-Group Society in the Context of Northeastern Africa."

58. Ehret, "The Establishment of Iron-Working in Eastern, Central, and Southern Africa."

59. Ehret, "Sudanic Civilization."

60. E.g., Ehret, "Africa—Equatorial and Southern Africa (4000 BCE–1100 CE)." For a recent, accessibly written survey of the social and cultural *longue durée* history of Bantu-speaking peoples, see Fourshey, Gonzales, and Saidi, *Bantu Africa: 3500 BCE to Present.*

61. Saxon, "Linguistic Evidence for the Eastward Spread of Ubangian Peoples."

62. Bellwood, "The Origins and Spread of Agriculture in the Indo-Pacific Region"; Blust, "Prehistory of the Austronesian-Speaking Peoples"; Ross, Pawley, and Osmond, *The Lexicon of Proto Oceanic*; see also Ehret, "Agricultural Origins."

63. Shady Solís, *La ciudad sagrada de Caral-Supe en los albores de la civilización en el Perú*; Haas, Creamer, and Ruiz, "Dating the Late Archaic Occupation of the Norte Chico Region in Peru"; see also Mann, *1491: New Revelations of the Americas before Columbus*, 199–212.

64. Weise, "Women and Trade in the Nupe-Borgu Region during the Nineteenth and Twentieth Centuries."

65. Bay, *Wives of the Leopard*, presents a highly informative history of female roles and institutions of power and influence and how they evolved in one especially important West African kingdom of the seventeenth through nineteenth centuries CE.

66. Saidi, in undertaking field and archival research for her book, *Women's Authority and Society in Early East-Central Africa*, encountered a variety of cases of female chiefs across this region in both the early colonial and the precolonial periods.

67. Saidi, *Women's Authority and Society in Early East-Central Africa.*

68. E.g., Stephens, *A History of African Motherhood*; see also Jimenez, "Rites of Reproduction," which, in contrast, traces the long-term reshaping of male roles and agency in society and economy in a different Bantu-speaking region farther south in Africa.

69. Weise, "Women and Trade in the Nupe-Borgu Region during the Nineteenth and Twentieth Centuries."

70. Holl, "Early West African Metallurgies," presents the indirect evidence for small states in the Aïr region of West Africa by or before 1000 BCE; the Nok

region of Nigeria seems probably to have been home to an early strong state during the first millennium BCE, with its wealth coming probably from trade in the metals found in its territories.

71. Vansina, "The Bells of Kings"; Vansina, *Paths in the Rainforests.*

72. Garrard, "Myth and Metrology."

73. Two important recent sources on this history of cultural encounter are Gordon, "Cultural Identity of the 25th Dynasty Rulers of Ancient Egypt in Context"; and Pope, *The Double Kingdom under Taharqo.*

74. Ehret, *The Civilizations of Africa*, 200, presents this case in more detail.

75. Schmidt, Curtis, and Teka, *The Archaeology of Ancient Eritrea.*

76. Vegder, "Horses in Africa." He shows that the words for horse—*so*, *siso*, and closely similar shapes—in languages all around the great bend of the Niger River and widely in Mali, where the route from Carthage via the Hoggar region would have had its terminus, can be derived from Punic *ssw*. His findings place the spread of horses across the Sahara in the centuries before the destruction of Carthagian political and commercial power by Rome.

77. Dunbar, *How Religion Evolved and Why It Endures*, offers thought-provoking proposals about how the increased population sizes and the growth in scale of societal and political groupings over the previous several thousand years led toward the new kinds and wider regional reach of systems of religious observance and allegiance.

78. Ehret, *An African Classical Age*, 273–81.

79. Nicolas, "Origine et valeur du vocabulaire désignant les xylophones africains."

80. For a fascinating survey of this history and its long-term background, see Kumar, "'The Single Most Astonishing Fact of Human Geography.'"

81. For just such an examination, see Manning, "'Civilization' in History and Ideology since 1800."

82. And, after all, that is what the term "civilization" originally referred to—a society with cities—as its derivation from Latin *civis*, "town, city," tells us.

83. For extended applications of this conceptualization in the case of African history, see Ehret, *The Civilizations of Africa.* The reader may find useful the fact each chapter begins (and/or sometimes ends) with an assessment of Africa's fit in world history during the historical era covered in the chapter.

Appendix

1. Schuenemann et al., "Ancient Egyptian Mummy Genomes Suggest an Increase of Sub-Saharan African Ancestry in Post-Roman Periods."

2. Most notoriously, Charles Gabriel Seligman, *The Races of Africa* (London: Thornton Butterworth, 1930); in the light of what we know now about human biology, this work is hardly more than a racist tract masquerading as scholarship. Oxford University Press and the International African Institute, to their mutual great discredit, reissued it in 1957 and again in 1967, well after its unscientific

nature had become widely recognized. Unfortunately, it is still in print and available online to the unsuspecting.

3. Jennifer L. Baker, Charles N. Rotimi, and Daniel Shriner, "Human Ancestry Correlates with Language and Reveals That Race Is Not an Objective Genomic Classifier," *Scientific Reports* 7, no. 1572 (2017): https://doi.org/10.1038/s41598-017-01837-7.

BIBLIOGRAPHY

Adams, William Y. "Doubts about the Lost Pharaohs." *Journal of Near Eastern Studies* 44 (1985): 185–92.

Allen, Nicholas J., Hilary Callan, Robin Dunbar, and Wendy James, eds. *Early Human Kinship: From Sex to Social Reproduction*. Oxford: Blackwell, 2008.

Ambrose, Stanley H. "Small Things Remembered: Origins of Early Microlithic Industries in Sub-Saharan Africa." *Archaeological Papers of the American Anthropological Association* 12, no. 1 (2002): 9–29.

Anthony, David W. *The Horse, the Wheel, and Language: How Bronze-Age Riders from the Eurasian Steppes Shaped the Modern World*. Princeton, NJ: Princeton University Press, 2007.

Arkell, A. J. *Early Khartoum: An Account of the Excavation of an Early Occupation Site Carried Out by the Sudan Government Antiquities Service in 1944–5*. Oxford: Oxford University Press, 1949.

Assefa, Shiferaw Alema. "Omotic Peoples and the Early History of Agriculture in Southern Ethiopia." PhD diss., University of California, 2011.

Aubert, M., A. Brumm, M. Ramli, T. Sutikna, E. W. Saptomo, B. Hakim, M. J. Morwood, G. D. van den Bergh, L. Kinsley, and A. Dosseto. "Pleistocene Cave Art from Sulawesi, Indonesia." *Nature* 514 (2014): 223–27.

Bader, Bettina. "Cultural Mixing in Egyptian Archaeology: The 'Hyksos' as a Case Study." *Archaeological Review from Cambridge* 28, no. 1 (2013): 257–86.

Bar-Yosef, Ofer. "The Dispersal of Modern Humans in Eurasia: A Cultural Interpretation." In Paul Mellars, Katie Boyle, Ofer Bar-Yosef, and Chris Stringer, eds., *Rethinking the Human Revolution: New Behavioural and Biological Perspectives on the Origin and Dispersal of Modern Humans*, 207–18. Cambridge: McDonald Institute, 2007.

———. "Pleistocene Connexions between Africa and Southwest Asia: An Archaeological Perspective." *African Archaeological Review* 5 (1987): 29–38.

Bar-Yosef, Ofer, Trina Arpin, Yan Pan, David Cohen, Paul Goldberg, Chi Zhang, and Xiaohong Wu. "Early Pottery at 20,000 Years Ago in Xianrendong Cave, China." *Science* 336 (2012): 1696–700.

Bay, Edna G. *Wives of the Leopard: Gender, Politics, and Culture in the Kingdom of Dahomey*. Charlottesville: University of Virginia Press, 1998.

Bedaux, Rogier Michel Alphons, J. Polet, K. Sanogo, and A. Schmidt, eds. *Recherches archéologiques à Dia dans le delta intérieur du Niger (Mali): Bilan des saisons de fouilles 1998–2003*. Leiden: CNWS Publications, 2005.

Beja-Pereira, Albano, Philip R. England, Nuno Ferrand, Steve Jordan, Amel Omer Bakhiet, Mohammed Abdalla, Marjan Mashkour, Jordi Jordana, Pierre

Taberlet, and Gordon Luikart. "African Origins of the Domestic Donkey." *Science* 304 (2004): 1781.

Bellwood, Peter. "The Origins and Spread of Agriculture in the Indo-Pacific Region." In D. Harris, ed., *The Origins and Spread of Agriculture and Pastoralism in Eurasia*, 465–98. London: UCL Press, 1996.

Bengtson, John. "How Do You Solve a Problem like Euskera?" *Romance Philology* 72 (2018): 15–33.

Bestock, Laurel. "The First Kings of Egypt: The Abydos Evidence." In Emily Teeter, ed., *Before the Pyramids: The Origins of Egyptian Civilization*, 137–44. Chicago: Oriental Institute of the University of Chicago, 2011.

Blench, Roger. *Archaeology and the African Past*. Lanham, MD: Altamira, 2006.

Blust, Robert A. "Prehistory of the Austronesian-Speaking Peoples: A View from Language." *Journal of World Prehistory* 9, no. 4 (1995): 453–510.

Boivin, Nicole, and Dorian Q. Fuller. "Shell Middens, Ships and Seeds: Exploring Coastal Subsistence, Maritime Trade and the Dispersal of Domesticates in and around the Ancient Arabian Peninsula." *Journal of World Prehistory* 22 (2009): 113–80.

Bramanti, B., M. G. Thomas, W. Haak, M. Unterlaender, P. Jores, K. Tambets, I. Antanaitis-Jacobs, et al. "Genetic Discontinuity between Local Hunter-Gatherers and Central Europe's First Farmers." *Science* 326 (2009): 137–40.

Brass, Michael. "Early North African Cattle Domestication and Its Ecological Setting." *Journal of World Prehistory* 31, no. 1 (2017): 81–115.

Brooks, Alison, and Sally McBrearty. "The Revolution That Wasn't: A New Interpretation of the Origin of Modern Human Behavior." *Journal of Human Evolution* 39 (2000): 453–563.

Brown, Cecil H. "The Development of Agriculture in Prehistoric Mesoamerica: The Linguistic Evidence." In J. E. Stalier and M. Carrasco, eds., *Pre-Columbian Foodways: Interdisciplinary Approaches to Food, Culture, and Markets in Mesoamerica*, 71–107. Berlin: Springer.

Browning, S. R., B. L. Browning, Y. Zhou, S. Tucci, and J. M. Akey. "Analysis of Human Sequence Data Reveals Two Pulses of Archaic Denisovan Admixture." *Cell* 173 (2018): 53–61.

Brunton, Guy, and Gertrude Caton-Thompson. *The Badarian Civilisation and Predynastic Remains near Badari*. London: British School of Archaeology in Egypt, 1928.

Bynon, James. "Berber and Chadic: The Lexical Evidence." In James Bynon, ed., *Current Progress in Afro-Asiatic Linguistics: Papers of the Third International Hamito-Semitic Congress, London, 1978*, 241–90. Amsterdam: J. Benjamins, 1984.

Chauvet, Jean-Marie, Eliette Brunel Deschamps, Christian Hillaire, Jean Clottes, and Paul Bahn. *Dawn of Art: The Chauvet Cave; The Oldest Known Paintings in the World*. New York: H. N. Abrams, 1996.

Chirikure, Shadreck. "Connections between Hinterland and Coastal Southern Africa." Paper presented at "The Routes of Medieval Africa 11th–17th Centuries," Paris, March 5–7, 2019.

Clark, J. D., and G. R. Prince. "Use-Wear in Later Stone Age Microliths from Laga Oda, Haraghi, Ethiopia and Possible Functional Interpretations." *Azania* 13 (1978): 101–10.

Clark, J. D., and M.A.J. Williams. "Recent Archaeological Research in Southeastern Ethiopia (1974–1975): Some Preliminary Results." *Annales d'Ethiopie* 11 (1978): 19–44.

Close, A. E. "Current Research and Recent Radiocarbon Dates from Northern Africa." *Journal of African History* 21 (1980): 145–67.

———. "Current Research and Recent Radiocarbon Dates from Northern Africa, II." *Journal of African History* 25 (1984): 1–24.

Clottes, Jean, and David Lewis-Williams. *The Shamans of Prehistory: Trance and Magic in the Painted Caves*. New York: Harry N. Abrams, 1998.

Dunbar, Robin. *How Religion Evolved and Why It Endures*. London: Penguin, 2022.

Ehret, Christopher. "Africa—Equatorial and Southern Africa (4000 BCE–1100)." In William H. McNeill, Jerry H. Bentley, David Christian, Ralph C. Croizier, J. R. McNeill, Heidi Roupp, and Judith P. Zinser, eds., *Africa in World History*, 8–13. Great Barrington, MA: Berkshire Publishing Group, 2011.

———. "Africa from 48,000 to 9500 BCE." In David Christian, ed., *Introducing World History (to 10,000 BCE)*, 362–93. *The Cambridge World History*, vol. 1. Cambridge: Cambridge University Press, 2015.

———. *An African Classical Age: Eastern and Southern Africa in World History, 1000 B.C. to A.D. 400*. Charlottesville: University of Virginia Press, 1998.

———. "The African Sources of Egyptian Culture and Language." In Josep Cervelló Autuori, ed., *África antigua: El antiguo Egipto, una civilización africana*, 121–28. Actas de la IX Semana de Estudios Africanos del Centre d'Estudis Africans de Barcelona. Barcelona, 2001.

———. "Agricultural Origins: What Linguistic Evidence Reveals." In Graeme Barker and Candice Goucher, eds., *A World with Agriculture*, 55–92. *The Cambridge World History*, vol. 2. Cambridge: Cambridge University Press, 2015.

———. "Berber Peoples in the Sahara and North Africa: Linguistic Historical Proposals." In Maria Gatto, David Mattingly, Nick Ray, and Martin Sterry, eds., *Burial, Migration and Identity in the Ancient Sahara and Beyond*, 464–94. Cambridge: Cambridge University Press, 2019.

———. *The Civilizations of Africa: A History to 1800*. 2nd ed. Charlottesville: University of Virginia Press, 2016.

———. "Deep-Time Historical Contexts of Crow and Omaha Systems: Perspectives from Africa." In Thomas R. Trautmann and Peter M. Whiteley, eds., *Crow-Omaha: New Light on a Classic Problem of Kinship Analysis*, 173–202. Tucson: University of Arizona Press, 2012.

Ehret, Christopher. "Early Humans: Tools, Language, Culture." In David Christian, ed., *Introducing World History (to 10,000 BCE)*, 339–61. *The Cambridge World History*, vol. 1. Cambridge: Cambridge University Press, 2015.

———. "The Establishment of Iron-Working in Eastern, Central, and Southern Africa: Linguistic Inferences on Technological History." *Sprache und Geschichte in Afrika* 16/17 (1995/96): 125–75.

———. *A Historical-Comparative Reconstruction of Nilo-Saharan*. Cologne: Rüdiger Köppe Verlag, 2001.

———. *History and the Testimony of Language*. Berkeley: University of California Press, 2011.

———. "Linguistic Archaeology." *African Archaeological Review* 29, no. 2 (2012): 109–30.

———. "Linguistic Evidence and the Origins of Food Production in Africa: Where Are We Now?" In Chris J. Stevens, Sam Nixon, Mary Anne Murray, and Dorian Q. Fuller, eds., *Archaeology of African Plant Use*, 233–42. Walnut Creek, CA: Left Coast Press, 2014.

———. "A Linguistic History of Cultivation and Herding in Northeastern Africa." In Ahmed G. Fahmy, S. Kahlheber, and A. C. D'Andrea, eds., *Windows on the African Past: Current Approaches to African Archaeobotany*, 3:185–208. Frankfurt am Main: Africa Magna Verlag, 2011.

———. "Linguistic Stratigraphies and Holocene History in Northeastern Africa." In Karla Kroeper, Marek Chlodnicki, and Michal Kobusieweicz, eds., *Archaeology of Early Northeastern Africa: In Memory of Lech Krzyżaniak*, 1019–55. Studies in African Archaeology, vol. 9. Posnan, Poland: Posnan Archaeological Museum, 2006.

———. "The Nilo-Saharan Background of Chadic." In Paul Newman and Larry Hyman, eds., *West African Linguistics: Studies in Honor of Russell G. Schuh*, 56–66. *Studies in African Linguistics*, suppl. 11. Columbus: Ohio State University, 2006.

———. "Nilo-Saharans and the Saharo-Sudanese Neolithic." In Thurstan Shaw, Paul Sinclair, Bassey Andah, and Alex Okpoko, eds., *The Archaeology of Africa: Food, Metals and Towns*, 104–25. London: Routledge, 1993.

———. "On the Antiquity of Agriculture in Ethiopia." *Journal of African History* 20 (1979): 161–77.

———. "Proto-Cushitic Reconstruction." *Sprache und Geschichte in Afrika* 8 (1987): 7–180.

———. "Reconstructing Ancient Kinship in Africa." In Nicholas J. Allen, Hilary Callan, Robin Dunbar, and Wendy James, eds., *Early Human Kinship: From Sex to Social Reproduction*, 200–231. Oxford: Blackwell, 2008.

———. *Reconstructing Proto-Afroasiatic (Proto-Afrasian): Vowels, Tone, Consonants, and Vocabulary*. Berkeley: University of California Press, 1995.

———. "Sub-Saharan Africa: Linguistics." In Immanuel Ness and Peter Bellwood, eds., *The Encyclopedia of Global Human Migration*, 1:96–106. Malden, MA: Wiley-Blackwell, 2013.

———. "Sudanic Civilization." In Michael Adas, ed., *Agricultural and Pastoral Societies in Ancient and Classical History*, 224–74. Philadelphia: Temple University Press, for the American Historical Association, 2001.

———. "Who Were the Rock Artists? Linguistic Evidence for the Holocene Populations of the Sahara." In Alfred Muzzolini and Jean-Loïc Le Quellec, eds., *Symposium 13d: Rock Art and the Sahara; Proceedings of the International Rock Art and Cognitive Archaeology Congress News95*. Turin: Centro Studi e Museo d'Arte Prehistorica di Pinerolo, 1999.

Ehret, Christopher, S.O.Y. Keita, and Stephen Brandt. "Afroasiatic Language Family and Its History." Unpublished paper presented online at a workshop, "Archaeology and Language," Max Planck Institute of the Science of Human History, Jena, Germany, November 18, 2021.

Ehret, Christopher, S.O.Y. Keita, and Paul Newman. "The Origins of Afroasiatic," *Science* 306 (2004): 1680–81.

Ehret, Christopher, and Merrick Posnansky. *The Archaeological and Linguistic Reconstruction of African History*. Berkeley: University of California Press, 1982.

Feathers, J. K., and E. Migliorini. "Luminescence Dating at Katanda—A Reassessment." *Quaternary Science Reviews* 20, nos. 5–9 (2001): 961–66.

Fourshey, Catherine Cymone, Rhonda M. Gonzales, and Christine Saidi. *Bantu Africa: 3500 BCE to Present*. Oxford: Oxford University Press, 2018.

Fuller, Dorian Q. "Agricultural Origins and Frontiers in South Asia: A Working Synthesis." *Journal of World Prehistory* 20, no. 1 (2006): 1–86.

Galetti, Mauro, Marcos Moleón, Pedro Jordano, Mathias M. Pires, Paulo R. Guimarães Jr., Thomas Pape, Elizabeth Nichols, et al. "Ecological and Evolutionary Legacy of Megafauna Extinctions." *Biological Reviews* 93, no. 2 (October 2017): 845–62.

Garrard, Timothy. *Akan Weights and the Gold Trade*. London: Longman, 1980.

———. "Myth and Metrology: The Early Trans-Saharan Gold Trade." *Journal of African History* 23 (1982): 443–61.

Gatto, Maria C., David J. Mattingly, Nick M. Ray, and Martin Sterry, eds. *Burials, Migration and Identity in the Ancient Sahara and Beyond*. Cambridge: Cambridge University Press, 2019.

Gordon, William. "Cultural Identity of the 25th Dynasty Rulers of Ancient Egypt in Context: Formulation, Negotiation and Expression." PhD diss., University of California at Los Angeles, 2009.

Gosselain, Oliver P. "Technology and Style: Potters and Pottery among the Bafia of Cameroon." *Man* 27, no. 3 (1992): 559–86.

Günther, Torsten, Cristina Valdiosera, Helena Malmström, Irene Ureña, Ricardo Rodriguez-Varela, Óddny Osk Sverrisdóttir, Evangelia A. Daskalaki, et al. "Ancient Genomes Link Early Farmers from Atapuerca in Spain to Modern-Day Basques." *Proceedings of the National Academy of Sciences* 112, no. 38 (2015): 11917–22.

Haas, Jonathan, Winifred Creamer, and Alvaro Ruiz. "Dating the Late Archaic Occupation of the Norte Chico Region in Peru." *Nature* 432, no. 7020 (2004): 1020–23.

Hassan, Fekri. "The Predynastic of Egypt." *Journal of World Prehistory* 2, no. 2 (1988): 135–85.

Henshilwood, Christopher S., Francesco d'Errico, and Ian Watts. "Engraved Ochres from the Middle Stone Age Levels at Blombos Cave, South Africa." *Journal of Human Evolution* 57, no. 1 (2009): 27–47.

Herbert, Eugenia. "Aspects of the Use of Copper in Pre-colonial West Africa." *Journal of African History* 14 (1973): 179–94.

——. *Red Gold of Africa: Copper in Precolonial History and Culture*. Madison: University of Wisconsin Press, 1984.

Herniter, Ira A., María Muñoz-Amatriaín, and Timothy J. Close. "Genetic, Textual, and Archaeological Evidence of the Historical Global Spread of Cowpea (*Vigna unguiculata* [L.] Walp)." *Legume Science* 2, no. 4 (2020): e57.

Hoffmann, D. L., C. D. Standish, M. García-Diez, P. B. Pettitt, J. A. Milton, J. Zilhão, J. J. Alcolea-González, et al. "U-Th Dating of Carbonate Crusts Reveals Neandertal Origin of Iberian Cave Art." *Science* 359 (2018): 912–15.

Holl, Augustin F. C. "Early West African Metallurgies: New Data and Old Orthodoxy." *Journal of World Prehistory* 22, no. 4 (2009): 415–38.

——. *Economie et société néolithique du dhar Tichitt, Mauritanie*. Paris: Editions Recherche sur les Civilisations, 1986.

——. *The Land of Houlouf: Genesis of a Chadic Polity, 1900 B.C.–A.D. 1800*. Ann Arbor, MI: Museum of Anthropology, 2002.

Hsieh, Ping Hsun, A. E. Woerner, J. Lachance, S. Tishkoff, J. D. Wall, R. N. Gutenkunst, and M. F. Hammer. "Model-Based Analyses of Whole-Genome Data Reveal a Complex Evolutionary History Involving Archaic Introgression in Central African Pygmies." *Genome Research* 26 (2016): 291.

Huysecom, E., M. Rasse, L. Lespez, K. Neumann, A. Fahmy, A. Ballouche, S. Ozainne, et al. "The Emergence of Pottery in Africa during the 10th Millennium calBC: New Evidence from Ounjougou (Mali)." *Antiquity* 83 (2009): 905–17.

Jimenez, Raevin. "Rites of Reproduction: Tradition, Political Ethics, Gender and Generation among Nguni-Speakers of Southern Africa, 8th–19th Century CE." PhD diss., Northwestern University, 2017.

Keita, S.O.Y. "Early Farmers from El-Badari: Aboriginals or 'European' Agro-Nostratic Immigrants to the Nile Valley? Craniometric Affinities Considered with Other Evidence." In Karla Kroeper, Marek Chlodnicki, and Michal Kobusieweicz, eds., *Archaeology of Early Northeastern Africa: In Memory of Lech Krzyz´aniak*, 751–65. Poznan, Poland: Poznan Archaeological Museum, 2006.

——. "Further Studies of Crania from Ancient Northern Africa: An Analysis of Crania from First Dynasty Egyptian Tombs, Using Multiple Discrimination Functions." *American Journal of Physical Anthropology* 87 (1992): 245–354.

———. "History in the Interpretation of the Pattern of p49a,f TaqI RFLP Y-Chromosome Variation in Egypt: A Consideration of Multiple Lines of Evidence." *American Journal of Human Biology* 17 (2005): 559–67.

———. "Studies of Ancient Crania from Northern Africa." *American Journal of Physical Anthropology* 83 (1990): 35–48.

Kelly, Robert L. *The Fifth Beginning: What Six Million Years of Human History Can Tell Us about Our Future.* Oakland: University of California Press, 2016.

Kimber, Clarissa T. "Origins of Domesticated Sorghum and Its Early Diffusion to India and China." In C. Wayne Smith and Richard A. Fredriksen, eds., *Sorghum: Origin, History, Technology, and Production*, 3–98. New York: John Wiley, 2000.

Kitchen, Andrew, Christopher Ehret, Shiferaw Assefa, and Connie Mulligan. "Bayesian Phylogenetic Analysis of Semitic Languages Identifies an Early Bronze Age Origin of Semitic in the Near East." *Proceedings of the Royal Society B: Biological Sciences* 276 (7 August 2009): 2703–10.

Klieman, Kairn. *"The Pygmies Were Our Compass": Bantu and Batwa in the History of West Central Africa, Early Times to c. 1900 C.E.* Portsmouth, NH: Heinemann, 2003.

Knight, Chris. "Early Human Kinship Was Matrilineal." In Nicholas J. Allen, Hilary Callan, Robin Dunbar, and Wendy James, eds., *Early Human Kinship: From Sex to Social Reproduction*, 61–82. Oxford: Blackwell Publishing, 2008.

Konner, Melvin, and Carol Worthman. "Nursing Frequency, Gonadal Function and Birth Spacing among !Kung Hunter-Gatherers." *Science* 207 (1980): 788–90.

Kriger, Colleen. "Mapping the History of Cotton Textile Production in Precolonial West Africa." *African Economic History* 33 (2005): 87–116.

Kroeper, Karla, Marek Chlodnicki, and Michal Kobusieweicz, eds. *Archaeology of Early Northeastern Africa: In Memory of Lech Krzyz´aniak.* Poznan, Poland: Poznan Archaeological Museum, 2006.

Krzyz'aniak, Lech. "Early Farming in the Middle Nile Basin: Recent Discoveries at Kadero." *Antiquity* 65 (2007): 515–32.

Kumar, Ann. "'The Single Most Astonishing Fact of Human Geography': Indonesia's Far West Colony." *Indonesia* 92 (October 2011): 59–96.

Kuper, Rudolf, and Stefan Kröpelin. "Climate-Controlled Holocene Occupation in the Sahara." *Science* 313 (2006): 803–7.

Kuzmin, Yaroslav. "The Paleolithic-to-Neolithic Transition and the Origin of Pottery Production in the Russian Far East: A Geoarchaeological Approach." *Archaeology, Ethnology & Anthropology of Eurasia* 3, no. 15 (2003): 16–26.

Lewis-Williams, J. David. *Seeing and Believing: Symbolic Meanings in Southern San Rock Paintings.* London: Academic Press, 1981.

Lienhardt, R. Godfrey. *Divinity and Experience: The Religion of the Dinka.* Oxford: Clarendon Press, 1961.

Madella, Marco, Juan José García-Granero, Welmoed A. Out, Philippa Ryan, and Donatella Usai. "Microbotanical Evidence of Domestic Cereals in Africa 7000 Years Ago." *PLOS ONE* 9, no. 10 (October 2014): 1–9.

Malville, J. McKim. "Astronomy at Nabta Playa, Southern Egypt." In Clive L. N. Ruggles, ed., *Handbook of Archaeoastronomy and Ethnoastronomy*, 2:1079–91. New York: Springer, 2015.

Malville, J. McKim, Romuald Schild, Fred Wendorf, and R. Brenmer. "Astronomy of Nabta Playa." *African Skies / Cieux Africains* 11 (2007): 2–7.

Mann, Charles C. *1491: New Revelations of the Americas before Columbus*. New York: Vintage Books, 2005.

Manning, Patrick. "'Civilization' in History and Ideology since 1800." *New Global Studies* 16, no. 3 (2022): 325–44.

———. *A History of Humanity: The Evolution of the Human System*. Cambridge: Cambridge University Press, 2020.

Manning, Patrick, with Tiffany Trimmer. *Migration in World History*. 3rd ed. New York: Routledge, 2020.

Marshall, Fiona. "Asses/Donkeys: Domestication." In Claire Smith, ed., *Encyclopedia of Global Archaeology*, 552–55. New York: Springer Reference, 2014.

Marshall, Fiona, and Elisabeth Hildebrand. "Cattle before Crops: The Beginnings of Food Production in Africa." *Journal of World Prehistory* 2, no. 16 (June 2002): 99–143.

Maschner, Herbert, and Owen K. Mason. "The Bow and Arrow in Northern North America." *Evolutionary Anthropology* 22 (2013): 133–38.

McCoy, R. C., J. Wakefield, and J. M. Akey. "Impact of Neandertal Introgressed Sequence on the Landscape of Human Gene Expression Variation." *Cell* 168 (2017): 916–27.

McIntosh, Roderick. *Ancient Middle Niger: Urbanism and the Self-Organizing Landscape*. Cambridge: Cambridge University Press, 2005.

———. *Peoples of the Middle Niger: The Island of Gold*. Malden, MA: Blackwell Publishers, 1998.

McIntosh, Susan Keech, ed. *Beyond Chiefdoms: Pathways to Complexity in Africa*. Cambridge: Cambridge University Press, 1999.

McIntosh, Susan Keech, and Roderick J. McIntosh. *Prehistoric Investigations in the Region of Jenne, Mali: A Study in the Development of Urbanism in the Sahel*. Oxford: B.A.R., 1980.

———. "Recent Archaeological Research and Dates from West Africa." *Journal of African History* 27 (1986): 413–42.

McMaster, Mary Allen. "Patterns of Interaction: A Comparative Ethnolinguistic Perspective on the Uele Region of Zaire, ca. 500 B.C. to 1900 A.D." PhD diss., University of California at Los Angeles, 1988.

McNaughton, Patrick. "The Throwing Knife in African History." *African Arts* 3, no. 2 (1970): 54–60, 89.

Midant-Reynes, Béatrix. *The Prehistory of Egypt*. Oxford: Blackwell Publishing, 2006.

Mitchell, Peter. *The Donkey in Human History: An Archaeological Perspective*. Oxford: Oxford University Press, 2018.

Moñino, Yves. *Le Proto-Gbaya: Essai de linguistique comparative historique sur vingt-et-une langues d'Afrique centrale*. Paris: Peters, 1995.

Mtetwa, Ezekial, Yananiso Chinovava Maposa, Munyaradzi Manyanga, and Shadreck Chirikure. "When the Smith Is a Woman: Innovation, Improvisation and Ambiguity in the Organisation of African Iron Metallurgy." In Munyaradzi Manyanga and Shadreck Chirikure, eds., *Archives, Object, Places and Landscapes: Multidisciplinary Approaches to Decolonise Zimbabwean Pasts*, 295–318. Bamenda, Cameroon: Langaa Research and Publishing Common Initiative Group, 2017.

Murphy, C. A., and Dorian Q Fuller. "Agricultural Origins and Frontiers in the Indian Subcontinent: A Current Synthesis." In Ravi Korisettar, ed., *Beyond Stones and More Stones*, 15–94. Bangalore: Mythic Society, 2017.

Newman, Paul. *The Classification of Chadic within Afroasiatic*. Leiden: Universitaire Pers, 1980.

Nicolas, Gildas. "The Dizzu of Southwest Ethiopia: An Essay in Cultural History Based on Religious Interactions." PhD diss., University of California at Los Angeles, 1976.

Nicolas, T. J. "Origine et valeur du vocabulaire désignant les xylophones africains." *Zaire* 11 (1957): 69–89.

Ogbomo, Onwaiwu. *When Men and Women Mattered: A History of Gender Relations among the Owan of Nigeria*. Rochester, NY: University of Rochester Press, 1997.

Ogundiran, Akinwumi. *The Yorùbá: A New History*. Bloomington: Indiana University Press, 2020.

Olszewski, D. I. "Issues in the Levantine Epipaleolithic: The Madamaghan, Nebekian and Qalkhan (Levant Epipaleolithic)." *Paléorient* 32, no. 1 (2006): 19–26.

Palmer, Sarah A., Alan J. Clapham, Pamela Rose, Fábio O. Freitas, Bruce D. Owen, David Beresford-Jones, Jonathan D. Moore, James L. Kitchen, and Robin G. Allaby. "Archaeogenomic Evidence of Punctuated Genome Evolution in *Gossypium*." *Molecular Biology and Evolution* 29, no. 8 (August 2012): 2031–38.

Pawley, Andrew. "The Chequered Career of the Trans New Guinea Hypothesis: Recent Research and Its Implications." In Andrew Pawley, Robert Attenborough, Robin Hide, and Jack Golson, eds., *Papuan Pasts: Cultural, Linguistic and Biological Histories of Papuan-Speaking Peoples*, 67–107. Canberra: Pacific Linguistics, 2005.

Pawley, Andrew, and Harald Hammarström. "The Trans New Guinea Family." In Bill Palmer, ed., *The Languages and Linguistics of the New Guinea Area: A Comprehensive Guide*, 21–196. The World of Linguistics 4. Berlin: De Gruyter Mouton, 2018.

Picton, John, and J. Mack. "The Classification and Distribution of Horizontal Treadle Looms in Sub-Saharan Africa." In Dale Idiens and K. G. Ponting, eds., *Textiles in Africa*. Bath: Pasold Research Fund, 1980.

Pleger, Thomas C. "Old Copper and Red Ocher Social Complexity." *Midcontinental Journal of Archaeology* 25 (2000): 169–90.

Pope, Jeremy. *The Double Kingdom under Taharqo: Studies in the History of Kush and Egypt, c. 690–664 BC.* Leiden: Brill, 2014.

Quiles, Anita, Hélène Valladas, Hervé Bocherens, Emmanuelle Delqué-Kolic, Evelyne Kaltnecker, Johannes van der Plicht, Jean-Jacques Delannoy, et al. "A High-Precision Chronological Model for the Decorated Upper Paleolithic Cave of Chauvet-Pont d'Arc, Ardèche, France." *Proceedings of the National Academy of Sciences* 113, no. 17 (1996): 4670–75.

Rahmani, Noura. *Le Capsien typique et le Capsien supérieur: Évolution ou contemporanéité; Les données technologiques.* Cambridge Monographs in Archaeology 57. Oxford: Archaeopress, 2003.

Rosette, J. P. "Les plus vieilles céramiques du Sahara (préhistoire du Niger)." *Archéologia* 183 (1985): 43–50.

Ross, Malcolm, Andrew Pawley, and Meredith Osmond, eds. *The Lexicon of Proto Oceanic: The Culture and Environment of Ancestral Oceanic Society.* Vol. 1, *Material Culture.* Canberra: Pacific Linguistics, Australian National University, 1998.

Saidi, Christine. *Women's Authority and Society in Early East-Central Africa.* Rochester, NY: University of Rochester Press, 2010.

Sandom, Christopher, Søren Faurby, Brody Sandel, and Jens-Christian Svenning. "Global Late Quaternary Megafauna Extinctions Linked to Human, Not Climate Change." *Proceedings of the Royal Society B* 281, no. 1787 (June 4, 2014): 20133254.

Sapir, Edward. *Time Perspective in Aboriginal American Culture: A Study in Method.* Ottawa: Government Printing Bureau, 1916.

Saxon, Douglas E. "Linguistic Evidence for the Eastward Spread of Ubangian Peoples." In C. Ehret and M. Posnansky, eds., *The Archaeological and Linguistic Reconstruction of African History,* 66–77. Berkeley: University of California Press, 1982.

Schild, Romuald, and Fred Wendorf. "The Megaliths of Nabta Playa." *Focus on Archeology* 1, no. 1 (2004): 9–15.

Schmidt, Peter R. *Historical Archaeology in Africa: Representation, Social Memory, and Oral Traditions.* Lanham, MD: AltaMira Press, 2006.

———. "Science in Africa: A History of Ingenuity and Invention in African Iron Technology." In W. H. Worger, C. Ambler, and N. Achebe, eds., *A Companion to African History,* 267–88. Hoboken, NJ: Wiley Blackwell, 2019.

Schmidt, Peter R., and Donald Avery. "Complex Iron Smelting and Prehistoric Culture in Tanzania." *Science* 201 (1978): 1085–89.

———. "More Evidence for an Advanced Prehistoric Iron Technology in Africa." *Journal of Field Archaeology* 10, no. 4 (1983): 421–34.

Schmidt, Peter R., Matthew C. Curtis, and Zelalem Teka, eds. *The Archaeology of Ancient Eritrea.* Trenton, NJ: Red Sea Press, 2008.

Schoenbrun, David L. *A Green Place, a Good Place: Agrarian Change, Gender, and Social Identity in the Great Lakes Region to the 15th Century*. Portsmouth, NH: Heinemann, 1998.

Schuenemann, V. J., A. Peltzer, B. Welte, W. P. van Pelt, M. Molak, C.-C. Wang, A. Furtwängler, et al. "Ancient Egyptian Mummy Genomes Suggest an Increase of Sub-Saharan African Ancestry in Post-Roman Periods." *Nature Communications* 8 (2017): 15694.

Shady Solís, Ruth Martha. *La ciudad sagrada de Caral-Supe en los albores de la civilización en el Perú*. Lima: UNMSM, Fondo Editorial, 1997.

Shaw, Thurstan, Paul Sinclair, Bassey Andah, and Alex Okpoko, eds. *The Archaeology of Africa: Food, Metals and Towns*. London: Routledge, 1993.

Shea, John J., and Matthew L. Sisk. "Complex Projective Technology and *Homo sapiens* Dispersal from Africa to Western Eurasia." *Paleoanthropology* (2010): 100–122.

Shiner, J. "The Cataract Tradition." In Fred Wendorf, ed., *The Prehistory of Nubia*, 2:535–629. Dallas: Southern Methodist University Press, 1968.

Sisk, Matthew L., and John Shea. "The African Origin of Complex Projectile Technology: An Analysis Using Tip Cross-Sectional Area and Perimeter." *International Journal of Evolutionary Biology*, article ID 968012 (2011): https://doi.org/10.4061/2011/968012.

Skoglund, P., H. Malmström, M. Raghavan, J. Storå, P. Hall, E. Willerslev, M.T.P. Gilbert, et al. "Origins and Genetic Legacy of Neolithic Farmers and Hunter-Gatherers in Europe." *Science* 336 (2012): 466–69.

Smith, Bruce D., and Richard A. Yarnell. "Initial Formation of an Indigenous Crop Complex in Eastern North America." *Proceedings of the National Academy of Sciences* 106, no. 16 (2009): 6561–66.

Smythe, Kathleen R. *Africa's Past, Our Future*. Bloomington: University of Indiana Press, 2015.

Stanton, Marsha A., J. McD. Stewart, A. Edward Percival, and Jonathan F. Wendel. "Morphological Diversity and Relationships in the A-Genome Cottons, *Gossypium arboreum* and *G. herbaceum*." *Crop Science* 34, no. 2 (March 1994): 519–27.

Stephens, Rhiannon. *A History of African Motherhood: The Case of Uganda, 700–1900*. Cambridge: Cambridge University Press, 2013.

Sterry, Martin, and David J. Mattingly, eds. *Urbanisation and State Formation in the Ancient Sahara and Beyond*. Cambridge: Cambridge University Press, 2020.

Stock, Frauke, and Diane Gifford-Gonzales. "Genetics and African Cattle Domestication." *African Archaeological Review* 30 (2013): 51–72.

Sutton, J.E.G. "The African Aqualithic." *Antiquity* 51 (1977): 25–34.

———. "The Aquatic Civilization of Middle Africa." *Journal of African History* 15 (1974): 527–46.

Teeter, Emily, ed. *Before the Pyramids: The Origins of Egyptian Civilization*. Chicago: Oriental Institute of the University of Chicago, 2011.

Tsutaya, Takumi, Akina Shimomi, Shiori Fujisawa, and Kazumichi Katazama. "Isotopic Evidence of Breastfeeding and Weaning Practices in a Hunter-Gatherer Population during the Late/Final Jomon Period in Eastern Japan." *Journal of Archaeological Science* 76 (December 2016): 70–78.

van der Kaars, Sander, Ellen Cook, Chris S. M. Turney, and Dirk Nuernberg. "Humans Rather Than Climate the Primary Cause of Pleistocene Megafaunal Extinction in Australia." *Nature Communications* 8 (2017): 14142.

Van Grunderbeek, Marie-Claude. "Essai de délimitation chronologique de l'Age du Fer Ancien au Burundi, au Rwanda et dans la région de Grands Lacs." *Azania* 28 (1992): 53–80.

Van Grunderbeek, Marie-Claude, E. Roche, and H. Doutrelepont. *Le premier age du fer au Rwanda et au Burundi.* Publication no. 23. Brussels: Institut National de Recherche Scientifique, 1983.

Vansina, Jan. "The Bells of Kings." *Journal of African History* 10, no. 2 (1969): 187–97.

———. *Children of Woot: A History of the Kuba Peoples.* Madison: University of Wisconsin Press, 1978.

———. *Évolution du royaume Rwanda des origines à 1900.* Brussels: Académie Royale des Sciences d'Outre-Mer, 2000.

———. *How Societies Are Born: Governance in West Central Africa before 1600.* Charlottesville: University of Virginia Press, 2004.

———. *Paths in the Rainforests: Toward a History of Political Tradition in Equatorial Africa.* Madison: University of Wisconsin Press, 1990.

———. "The Use of Ethnographic Data as Sources for History." In T. O. Ranger, ed., *Emerging Themes of African History*, 97–124. London: Heinemann, 1968.

———. "The Use of Process Models in African History." In Jan Vansina, L. V. Thomas, and Raymond Mauny, eds., *The Historian in Tropical Africa*, 375–89. London: International African Institute, 1964.

Vegder, Jerold. "Horses in Africa." Unpublished seminar paper, University of California at Los Angeles, 1980.

Waite, Gloria Martha. *A History of Traditional Medicine and Health Care in Precolonial Central Africa.* Lewiston, NY: E. Mellen Press, 1992.

Webb, James L. A., Jr. *Humanity's Burden: The Global History of Malaria.* Cambridge: Cambridge University Press, 2009.

Weise, Constanze. "Governance and Ritual Sovereignty at the Niger-Benue Confluence: A Political and Cultural History of Nigeria's Igala, Northern Yoruba and Nupoid-Speaking Peoples to 1900 CE." PhD diss., University of California, 2013.

———. "Women and Trade in the Nupe-Borgu Region during the Nineteenth and Twentieth Centuries." *Canadian Journal of African Studies / Revue Canadienne des Études Africaines* 54, no. 3 (2020): https://doi.org/10.1080/00083968.2020.1749097.

Welsby, Derek A. *The Kingdom of Kush: The Napatan and Meroitic Empires.* Princeton, NJ: Markus Wiener Publishers, 1998.

Wendorf, Fred, and Romuald Schild. "Are the Early Holocene Cattle in the Eastern Sahara Domestic or Wild?" *Evolutionary Anthropology* 3, no. 4 (1995): 118–28.

———. *The Prehistory of the Eastern Sahara.* New York: Academic Press, 1980.

———. *Prehistory of the Nile Valley.* New York: Academic Press, 1976.

Wendt, W. E. "'Art Mobilier' from the Apollo 11 Cave, South West Africa: Africa's Oldest Dated Works of Art." *South African Archaeological Bulletin* 31 (1976): 5–11.

Wengrow, David, Michael Dee, Sarah Foster, Alice Stevenson, and Christopher Bronk Ramsey. "Cultural Convergence in the Neolithic of the Nile Valley: A Prehistoric Perspective on Egypt's Place in Africa." *Antiquity* 88 (2014): 95–111.

Wetterstrøm, Wilma. "Foraging and Farming in Egypt: The Transition from Hunting and Gathering to Horticulture in the Nile Valley." In T. Shaw et al., *The Archaeology of Africa*, 165–226. London: Routledge, 1993.

Williams, Bruce B. "A-Group Society in the Context of Northeastern Africa." In Karla Kroeper, Marek Chlodnicki, and Michal Kobusieweicz, eds., *Archaeology of Early Northeastern Africa: In Memory of Lech Krzyz'aniak*, 177–94. Poznan, Poland: Poznan Archaeological Museum, 2006.

———. "Forebears of Menes in Nubia, Myth or Reality?" *Journal of Near Eastern Studies* 46 (1987): 15–26.

———. "The Lost Pharaohs of Nubia: Reevaluating the Cemetery and Evidence from Qustul." *Archaeology* 33, no. 5 (1980): 12–21.

———. "Relations between Egypt and Nubia in the Naqada Period." In Emily Teeter, ed., *Before the Pyramids: The Origins of Egyptian Civilization*, 81–92. Chicago: Oriental Institute of the University of Chicago, 2011.

Zakrzewski, Sonia R. "Population Continuity or Population Change: Formation of the Ancient Egyptian State." *American Journal of Physical Anthropology* 132 (2007): 501–9.

Zangato, E. *Les ateliers d'Ôboui: Premières communautés métallurgistes dans le nord-ouest du Centrafrique.* Paris: Editions Recherche sur les Civilisations, 2007.

Zangato, E., and A.F.C. Holl. "On the Iron Front: New Evidence from Central Africa." *Journal of African Archaeology* 8 (2010): 7–23.

Zhushchikhovskaya, Irina. *Prehistoric Pottery-Making of the Russian Far East.* Translated and edited by Richard L. Bland and C. Melvin Aikens. Oxford: Archaeopress, 2005.

INDEX

Page numbers in *italics* refer to tables, maps, and illustrations.